ALLERGEN-FREE DESSERTS TO DELIGHT YOUR TASTE BUDS

ALLERGEN-FREE DESSERTS TO DELIGHT YOUR TASTE BUDS

A BOOK FOR PARENTS AND KIDS

AMANDA ORLANDO

Skyhorse Publishing

Skyhorse Publishing books may be purchased in bulk at special discounts for sales promotion, corporate gifts, fund-raising, or educational purposes. Special editions can also be created to specifications. For details, contact the Special Sales Department, Skyhorse Publishing, 307 West 36th Street, 11th Floor, New York, NY 10018 or info@skyhorsepublishing.com.

Skyhorse® and Skyhorse Publishing® are registered trademarks of Skyhorse Publishing, Inc.®, a Delaware corporation.

Visit our website at www.skyhorsepublishing.com.

10 9 8 7 6 5 4 3 2 1

Library of Congress Cataloging-in-Publication Data is available on file.

Cover design by Mary Belibasakis
Cover photo credit: Amanda Orlando

ISBN: 978-1-63220-337-3
Ebook ISBN: 978-1-63220-787-6
Printed in China

DEDICATION

For Aunt Marilyn

Table of Contents

❖ ACKNOWLEDGMENTS

First of all thank you to my brother for tasting every single recipe in this book multiple times, especially within the last few years. Humans everywhere envy your metabolism. Thank you to Brandon for your love and encouragement when I was feeling overwhelmed and unable to look at sugar anymore. Thank you to my parents for trusting me to use the stove as soon as I was old enough to reach it and for tasting the many strange "creations" I came up with as a kid. Also, thank you for my first camera, this book wouldn't have been possible without it.

Thank you Karrie, Joella, Maddie, and Rya for volunteering to be my professional taste testers and for the positive encouragement! Although I'm finished writing the book, the care packages will still keep coming. Karrie especially, thanks for being an amazing best friend and providing me with mounds of support. Thank you Michael and Nicole for being fantastic models!

Thank you so much Bruce for writing the foreword, I really appreciate that you took the time to do that. Many thank you's to my agent, Haskell Nussbaum, and my editor, Catherine Kovach, who made this all possible. Thank you to Sarah Labrie, Kelvin Kong, Jason Hackworth, Jenny Lass, and Stella Grasso for the professional advice.

To all my friends and family, thank you for your ambitious and gracious support! From the moment I found out that my dream of becoming an author was becoming a reality, I was overwhelmed with congratulatory emails, calls, and messages of pride and promise to support my work. I truly appreciate it.

FOREWORD

Thank you, Amanda, for putting this very valuable cookbook together. Speaking for those of us whose families live with food allergies, I appreciate any resource that helps with this day-to-day challenge. Food is the spice of life and this book is full of healthy, safe alternatives. Delicious!!!

Bruce Croxon

Bake sales are a fun and tasty tradition at elementary schools all over, but not necessarily so for kids who have food allergies. Usually restricted to the baked goods prepared by their parents, allergic kids are not able to fully enjoy the ritual of lining up single file and marching over to the bake sale, tables lined with proud moms and delicious treats. Birthday parties and classroom parties are a similar story. Oftentimes, children with allergies will feel left out of the experience because they cannot fully or as freely participate or interact in social situations involving food. When one of the highlights of a party is the big birthday cake or the table of treats, it is hard for kids who are allergic to those things to get excited or feel included. The effects of food allergies are not simply physical; it is important to remember that they also affect children emotionally and psychologically. The goal of this cookbook is to promote inclusivity at home and at school, and to help parents and children who do not have allergies discover that allergen-free baking is a simple and delicious way to promote social inclusion and understanding.

I'd like you to know that I am speaking from personal experience. I have had severe allergies to dairy, nuts, peanuts, legumes, and high concentrations of soy, for my whole life. As many parents know, schools are now taking precautionary measures to reduce the threat of reaction by banning peanuts, nuts, and other common allergens. A measure that allergic kids (the numbers of which are on the rise) greatly appreciate.

I understand that this can be difficult to accommodate for someone who has never encountered food allergies before, and that many find it a contentious issue to tiptoe around.

If you've picked up this book I think it's pretty safe to assume that you or someone you know has food allergies or intolerances. Maybe you're a pro at being an allergy parent, or maybe dietary restrictions are a whole new experience for you. Either way, I hope you find this book to be a helpful and delicious tool to add to your allergen-free repertoire. For someone new to the allergen-free scene, it's hard to know what exactly contains gluten or dairy, if nutmeg is actually a nut, or if coconut milk and butternut squash are hereby barred from the school on two counts of threatening an allergic reaction. That's why I have included allergen information for each recipe, so that you and your kids can be confident in the kitchen without having to question each ingredient.

It is understandable that people who are not accustomed to food allergies will shy away from allergy-friendly baking. If you've abandoned the idea of baking something yourself for your child's birthday, class party, or bake sale, you may decide to buy something "allergy friendly" from the store. After picking up any box in the grocery store you will probably come to realize that packaged foods are laced with various dairy, wheat, corn, and nut products. Even in small amounts these ingredients can be very dangerous for a person with allergies. You may come to find products that claim they are allergy friendly but still do contain many common allergens (oh the lies!). Understandably, this can leave you stumped. How do I make substitutions in my decadent-French-pastries cookbook to accommodate the kids with allergies to dairy and nuts?

Do not despair! I have taken the liberty of putting together a quick guide to baking using simple and fun recipes that you can do with your kids and that will impress at any event, and that can fool the taste buds of the masses. This collection of recipes is a great resource for kids or families with allergies to dairy, nuts, peanuts, legumes, eggs, and citrus. All of the following recipes were designed for kids to do with their parents—a great alternative to watching TV or sitting online. They are laid out in a clear, easy-to-follow way, so that even your kids can take charge of the kitchen!

Before you begin your baking adventure, here are some helpful tips . . .

First, I advise that you inform yourself of the allergens that are off-limits in your school, and if any of your kids' friends have any other allergies that have not been banned but may be life-threatening to them (this will also be helpful when birthday parties roll around). It's best to write them down so you can refer to them at any time and have them at the ready for when your kids tell you at 11:54 p.m. that you have to bake 35 cupcakes for their class the next morning. It is also a good idea to search the allergens online to see if they go by any other names, and to see which foods commonly contain them. The more you familiarize yourself, the more comfortable you will become with avoiding them. For example, dairy can also go by the names lactose, whey powder, modified milk ingredients, and casein, but contrary to popular thought, eggs are not considered dairy. Gluten-free products can also be tricky because many gluten substitutes are made of nuts or legumes, such as almond or pea flour.

Another step you should take to ensure that your efforts aren't all for naught, is to clean down the space in which you will be baking. Wiping down utensils, bowls, counters, and other surfaces with a new sponge will help prevent cross contamination from allergen residues.

Once you have decided what you are going to bake and you arrive at the grocery store to buy your ingredients, make sure you read all the labels to confirm they are free of the allergens and don't have any disclaimers, for example—that they may contain or were produced on the same equipment as the allergen. People with serious allergies generally do not take chances when disclaimers are put on packages, so neither should you. It is better to sacrifice a certain flavor, design, or recipe altogether than to take a chance buying something that "may contain" offensive allergens.

Finally, keep a list of the ingredients you used with you at the bake sale, birthday party, or other event. Kids with allergies are often more comfortable reading the ingredients for themselves (or for small children, letting their parents read the ingredients) to confirm it's okay for them, or to check if any other allergens they must avoid are on the list that might not have been banned from the school. It's important to remember it's not enough to say something is "allergy friendly."

That doesn't mean it's free of every allergen or that it's free of the particular allergens that person is allergic to. But, with some careful steps and precautions, baked goods can be made safe and delicious for all to enjoy.

FROM THE FREEZER

Ice cream is universally one of the most popular desserts to enjoy in the summer. In fact, the number one thing people say to me when they discover that I'm allergic to dairy is "oh my God, does that mean you can't have ice cream?!" followed by a look of shock and dismay. I have never had "regular" ice cream; however, I have had a ton of sorbet and gelato over the years from a number of different brands. My favorites are the ones made with coconut milk, which I am told tastes just like the real thing (I'll have to take their word for it). Although there are many brands of dairy- and nut-free frozen desserts available, they tend to be expensive and can be difficult to find with any regularity. In this chapter you will learn how to make a selection of my favorite frozen desserts ranging from fruit-based to coconut milk-based. I promise these recipes will bring smiles to your kids' faces on a hot summer day.

Banana Chocolate Chip Soft Serve

Allergen Information
This recipe does not call for any dairy, nuts, peanuts, egg, citrus, or gluten.

Tools You Will Need
Standard 2 quart countertop ice cream maker
Blender
Measuring cup
Small saucepan
Whisk
Ice cream scooper

Ingredients
½ cup sugar
½ cup water
1 tsp pure vanilla extract
Pinch of salt
1 cup Coconut Dream
4 ripe bananas
⅓ cup Enjoy Life mini chocolate chips

Method
1. Chill the drum of your ice cream maker ahead of time according to package directions.
2. Peel the bananas and break each into smaller chunks that your blender can easily grind. Set aside.
3. Add the sugar and water to a small saucepan and turn the heat to medium. Allow the water to come to a boil, then immediately reduce the heat to low and let simmer for 15 minutes. This is called the simple syrup.
4. Add the simple syrup, vanilla, salt, Coconut Dream, and chunks of banana to the blender. Blend until the mixture is completely smooth.
5. Pour the blended mixture into your prepared ice cream maker and allow it to churn for 45 minutes. Halfway through you can stop the machine and pour in the chocolate chips. If you prefer the ice cream to be a bit firmer you can scoop it into a freezer strength plastic zipper bag and freeze for 15 – 20 minutes.
6. Serve using an ice cream scoop.

Serves 4 – 6

Coconut Ice Cream

Allergen Information

This recipe does not call for any dairy, nuts, peanuts, citrus, or gluten.

Tools You Will Need

Standard 2 quart countertop ice cream maker

Measuring cup

Medium saucepan

Whisk

Plastic spatula

Ice cream scooper

Ingredients

¾ cup sugar

3 tbsp honey

½ tsp pure vanilla extract

2 cups Coconut Dream

2 egg yolks

5 heaping tbsp of the fat from a tin of coconut milk

1 ½ cups shredded coconut

Method

1. Chill the drum of your ice cream maker ahead of time according to package directions.
2. Add the sugar, honey, vanilla, Coconut Dream, and egg yolks to a medium saucepan. Whisk until the egg yolks are well combined. The mixture may become a bit frothy on top.
3. Turn the stove on to medium heat and add the coconut fat, whisking continuously. If you stop whisking, the eggs may separate, leaving you with a scrambled mess.
4. Once all the coconut fat has been whisked in and no chunks remain, reduce the heat to low and allow to simmer for 15 minutes, still stirring continuously but with less vigor than before.
5. After 15 minutes remove the pot from the heat and allow it to come to room temperature.
6. Pour the mixture into your prepared ice cream maker and allow it to churn for 35 minutes. Halfway through you can stop the machine and scrape the bottom and sides with a plastic spatula. If you prefer the ice cream to be a bit firmer you can scoop it into a freezer strength plastic zipper bag and freeze for 15 – 20 minutes.
7. Serve using an ice cream scoop.

Serves 4 – 6

Strawberry Sorbet

Allergen Information
This recipe does not call for any dairy, nuts, peanuts, egg, citrus, or gluten.

Tools You Will Need
Standard 2 quart countertop ice cream maker
Blender
Measuring cup
Small saucepan
Paring knife
Cutting board
Ice cream scooper

Ingredients
1 lb strawberries
½ cup sugar
½ cup water

Method
1. Chill the drum of your ice cream maker ahead of time according to package directions.
2. Remove the stems from the strawberries. Set aside.
3. Add the sugar and water to a small sauce pan and turn the heat to medium. Allow the water to come to a boil, then immediately reduce the heat to low and let simmer for 15 minutes. This is called the simple syrup.
4. Add the simple syrup and strawberries to the blender. Blend until the mixture is completely smooth.
5. Pour the blended mixture into your prepared ice cream maker and allow it to churn for 25 minutes. If you prefer the ice cream to be a bit firmer you can scoop it into a freezer strength plastic zipper bag and freeze for 15 – 20 minutes.
6. Serve using an ice cream scoop.

Serves 3 – 5

Chocolate Chip Cookie Dough Ice Cream

Allergen Information
This recipe does not call for any dairy, nuts, citrus, or peanuts.

Tools You Will Need
Large mixing bowl
Large fork or electric mixer
Measuring cups and spoons
Plastic wrap
Spoon
Whisk
Standard 2 quart countertop ice cream maker
Medium saucepan

Ingredients

Cookie dough
½ cup shortening or vegan butter
½ cup demerara or dark brown sugar
¼ cup sugar
Pinch of salt
1 large egg
½ tsp vanilla
¾ cup + 1 heaping tbsp flour
¹/₃ cup Enjoy Life chocolate chips

Ice cream
¾ cup sugar
3 tbsp honey
½ tsp pure vanilla extract
2 cups Coconut Dream
2 egg yolks
5 heaping tbsp of the fat from a tin of coconut milk

Method

1. First prepare the base for the ice cream. Add the sugar, honey, vanilla, Coconut Dream, egg, and coconut milk fat to a medium saucepan and whisk well, making sure the egg yolk is fully combined.
2. When it's all whisked together you can put the pot on the stove and turn the heat to medium-high. Bring the mixture to a boil, whisking the whole time. When it reaches a boil turn the heat down to low immediately and let simmer for 15 minutes.
3. After 15 minutes remove the pot from the heat and let it come to room temperature before pouring into your ice cream maker.
4. Turn the ice cream maker on and let it churn the ice cream for 35 minutes.
5. While the ice cream is churning, you can prepare the cookie dough.
6. In a large bowl cream the vegan butter, sugar, and salt until smooth. You can use a large fork to do this, or an electric mixer on high speed.
7. Add the vanilla and egg and beat until well combined.
8. Add the flour and mix until the dough comes together in a ball and there are no lumps of flour remaining.
9. Fold in the chocolate chips with a spoon or with your mixer on low.
10. Dump the dough onto a sheet of parchment paper and wrap it up, then freeze for an hour.
11. When the ice cream is finished churning, scoop it out into a mixing bowl. Pull the chilled dough out of the freezer and chop it into cubes. There is no right or wrong way to do this, just make the chunks bite-sized. Pour them into the ice cream and fold it all together using a spatula.
12. Serve using an ice cream scoop.

Serves 8

Peach Sorbet

Allergen Information
This recipe does not call for any dairy, nuts, peanuts, egg, citrus, or gluten.

Tools You Will Need
Standard 2 quart countertop ice cream maker
Blender
Measuring cup
Small saucepan
Paring knife
Cutting board
Ice cream scooper

Ingredients
1 lb ripe peaches, peeled and pits removed
½ cup sugar
½ cup water

Method
1. Chill the drum of your ice cream maker ahead of time according to package directions.
2. Remove the pits from the peaches by slicing around the outside and twisting the two halves apart, then dig out the pit using a paring knife. Use a vegetable peeler to remove the skin. Cut the halves into chunks and set aside.
3. Add the sugar and water to a small saucepan and turn the heat to medium. Allow the water to come to a boil, then immediately reduce the heat to low and let simmer for 15 minutes. This is called the simple syrup.
4. Add the simple syrup and peaches to the blender. Blend until the mixture is completely smooth. There will be little bits of peach flesh visible, but that's all right. It gives the sorbet some added nutrients and texture.
5. Pour the blended mixture into your prepared ice cream maker and allow it to churn for 25 minutes. If you prefer the ice cream to be a bit firmer you can scoop it into a freezer strength plastic zipper bag and freeze for 15 – 20 minutes.
6. Serve using an ice cream scoop.

Serves 3 – 5

Fruit Punch Sorbet

Allergen Information
This recipe does not call for any dairy, nuts, peanuts, egg, or gluten.

Tools You Will Need
Standard 2 quart countertop ice cream maker
Blender
Measuring cup
Small saucepan
Zester/grater
Paring knife
Cutting board
Ice cream scooper

Ingredients
2 ripe mangoes, peeled and pits removed
1 lb strawberries
Zest of one orange
2 bananas
1 cup sugar
1 cup water
1 tbsp honey

Method
1. Chill the drum of your ice cream maker ahead of time according to package directions.
2. Prepare the fruit by removing the stems from the strawberries, removing the pit and skin from the mango, and removing the peel from the banana. Cut the bananas and mangoes up into 1 inch cubes to ease the job of the blender. Set the fruit aside.
3. Add the sugar and water to a small saucepan and turn the heat to medium. Allow the water to come to a boil, then immediately reduce the heat to low and let simmer for 15 minutes. This is called the simple syrup.
4. Grate the zest using a medium-grain zester. Add the simple syrup, honey, strawberries, bananas, mangoes, and orange zest to the blender. Blend until the mixture is completely smooth.
5. Pour the blended mixture into your prepared ice cream maker and allow it to churn for 30 minutes. If you prefer the ice cream to be a bit firmer you can scoop it into a freezer strength plastic zipper bag and freeze for 15 – 20 minutes.
6. Serve using an ice cream scoop.

Serves 6 – 8

Raspberry Sorbet

Allergen Information
This recipe does not call for any dairy, nuts, peanuts, egg, citrus, or gluten.

Tools You Will Need
Standard 2 quart countertop ice cream maker
Blender
Measuring cup
Small saucepan
Ice cream scooper
Tight-netted strainer
Large bowl
Spatula

Ingredients
1 lb raspberries
¾ cup sugar
½ cup water
2 tbsp honey

Method
1. Chill the drum of your ice cream maker ahead of time according to package directions.
2. Add the sugar and water to a small saucepan and turn the heat to medium. Allow the water to come to a boil, then immediately reduce the heat to low and let simmer for 15 minutes. This is called the simple syrup.
3. Add the simple syrup, honey, and raspberries to the blender. Blend until the mixture is completely smooth. Pass the mixture through a tight strainer set on top of a bowl before pouring into the ice cream maker. Use a spatula or spoon to press it through the strainer.
5. Pour the blended mixture into your prepared ice cream maker and allow it to churn for 30 minutes. If you prefer the ice cream to be a bit firmer you can scoop it into a freezer strength plastic zipper bag and freeze for 15 – 20 minutes.
6. Serve using an ice cream scoop.

Serves 3 – 5

Chocolate Ice Cream

Allergen Information
This recipe does not call for any dairy, nuts, peanuts, egg, citrus, or gluten.

Tools You Will Need
Measuring cups and spoons
Medium saucepan
Whisk
Standard 2 quart countertop ice cream maker

Ingredients
1 ¼ cups Coconut Dream
3 heaping tbsp of the fat from a tin of coconut milk
¾ cup Enjoy Life chocolate chunks
3 tbsp honey
Pinch of salt

Method
1. Chill the drum of your ice cream maker ahead of time according to package directions.
2. Add the Coconut Dream, coconut fat, chocolate chunks, honey, cocoa, and salt to a medium saucepan and turn to medium-low heat.
3. Whisk the mixture continuously until all the chocolate has melted and it is well combined. Then turn the heat down to low and allow it to simmer for 10 minutes, stirring constantly to prevent a skin from forming on top.
4. After 10 minutes remove the saucepan from the heat and allow it to come to room temperature.
5. When it has reached room temperature you can pour it into your prepared ice cream maker and allow it to churn for 35 minutes. If you prefer the ice cream to be a bit firmer you can scoop it into a freezer strength plastic zipper bag and freeze for 10 – 15 minutes.
6. Serve using an ice cream scoop.

Serves 4 – 6

Melon Pops

Allergen Information
This recipe does not call for any dairy, nuts, peanuts, egg, or gluten.

Tools You Will Need
Blender
Popsicle molds
Paring knife
Cutting board
Measuring cups and spoons

Ingredients
1 ½ cups peeled and diced honeydew melon (seeds removed)
1 tsp chopped mint
Juice of 1 lime
3 tbsp sugar
½ cup water or orange juice

Method
1. Remove the peel from the melon and then cut the flesh into cubes that will fit in your blender.
2. Add the lime juice, sugar, mint, water or orange juice and melon to the blender.
3. Blend until the mixture is completely smooth.
4. Pour into your Popsicle molds and freeze for at least 5 hours (preferably overnight).
5. Depending on the shape of your Popsicle mold, it may be easier to let them sit on the counter for 10 minutes before popping them out to allow them to loosen. Try to use a Popsicle mold that has a simple shape, as thin bits or points can be difficult to wiggle loose.

Makes 6 Popsicles

Mango Sorbet

Allergen Information
This recipe does not call for any dairy, nuts, peanuts, egg, citrus, or gluten.

Tools You Will Need
Standard 2 quart countertop ice cream maker

Blender

Measuring cup

Small saucepan

Paring knife

Cutting board

Ice cream scooper

Ingredients
3 cups diced mango

½ cup sugar

½ cup water

Method
1. Chill the drum of your ice cream maker ahead of time according to package directions.
2. Remove the pits from the mangoes by standing the mango up tall, then sliding your paring knife down the top until you feel the pit. The pit is long and flat, so you can just ride the knife along the edge of the pit all the way down to the bottom. Do this on either side of the pit and then proceed to peel off the skin with a paring knife. Cut the mango flesh into chunks and set aside.
3. Add the sugar and water to a small saucepan and turn the heat to medium. Allow the water to come to a boil, then immediately reduce the heat to low and let simmer for 15 minutes. This is called the simple syrup.
4. Add the simple syrup and mangoes to the blender. Blend until the mixture is completely smooth.
5. Pour the blended mixture into your prepared ice cream maker and allow it to churn for 25 minutes. If you prefer the ice cream to be a bit firmer you can scoop it into a freezer strength plastic zipper bag and freeze for 15 – 20 minutes.
6. Serve using an ice cream scoop.

Serves 3 – 5

Soda Float

This recipe does not call for any dairy, nuts, peanuts, egg, or gluten.

Tools You Will Need
2 large glasses
Ice cream scoop

Ingredients
1 batch of ice cream or sorbet
1 can of soda

Method
You can make your very own soda float at home by scooping a big helping (about $1/3$ cup) of ice cream or sorbet into a glass and then topping it up with a complementary soda. Some great combinations? Root beer and coconut ice cream, cherry cola and chocolate ice cream, peach or mango sorbet and ginger ale, all make great combinations! How about adding some orange zest to fruity soda floats to give them an extra boost of flavor? Try making mini soda floats in small glasses with your friends so you can each try them all.

Fruity Popsicles

This recipe does not call for any dairy, nuts, peanuts, egg, or gluten.

Tools You Will Need
Blender
Popsicle molds
Paring knife
Cutting board
Measuring cups and spoons

Ingredients
¼ cup strawberries
¼ cup peeled pineapple
¼ cup blueberries
½ cup fruit juice
½ cup water

Method
1. Remove the peel from the pineapple and then cut the flesh into cubes that will fit in your blender. Cut the stems off the strawberries and cut the strawberries into quarters.
2. Add the pineapple, strawberries, blueberries, juice, and water to the blender.
3. Blend until the mixture is completely smooth.
4. Pour into your Popsicle molds and freeze for at least 5 hours (preferably overnight).
5. Depending on the shape of your Popsicle mold, it may be easier to let them sit on the counter for 10 minutes before popping them out to allow them to loosen. Or you can try running each Popsicle quickly under hot water to loosen. Try to use a Popsicle mold that has a simple shape, as thin bits or points can be difficult to wiggle loose.

Makes 6 Popsicles

SWEET BREADS AND MUFFINS

What would a dessert cookbook be without the basics; zucchini bread, banana bread, carrot muffins, and some new savory-sweet combinations like olive oil herb or chocolate cinnamon muffins? I remember making zucchini bread with my parents, and let me tell you, accidentally doubling the amount of lemon zest can really spoil the batch! But it makes for some funny memories.

Olive Oil and Herb Muffins

This muffin is both savory and sweet. Olive oil cake is a common Italian baked good that is served a little differently depending on the region you come from. It has sweet notes of citrus and the rich taste of olive oil. Coming from the region of Toronto, I always liked to customize my version with the herbs my parents grew in the backyard. There's something wholesome about taking ingredients straight from the soil to the kitchen; however, I call for dried herbs in this recipe because if you're baking this on the fly or if it's not summer, you likely won't have fresh herbs around. These muffins are wonderful for breakfast with a glass of juice.

Allergen Information
This recipe does not call for any dairy, nuts, peanuts, or egg.

Tools You Will Need
Muffin pan and paper liners
Large mixing bowl
Whisk
Measuring cups and spoons
Spoon

Ingredients

¼ cup orange juice

¼ cup lemon juice

1 cup applesauce

½ cup olive oil

2 tbsp vegetable oil

A pinch of salt

1 tsp dried ground rosemary

½ tsp ground dried thyme

¼ tsp ground black pepper

½ tsp dried ground sage

1 ½ cups flour

¼ cup confectioner's sugar

2 tsp baking soda

1 tsp baking powder

Method

1. Preheat oven to 375F and line a muffin tray with paper muffin liners.
2. In a large bowl whisk the orange juice, lemon juice, applesauce, olive oil, vegetable oil, salt, rosemary, thyme, pepper, and sage together until well combined.
3. Add the flour, sugar, baking powder, and baking soda together and whisk well, until there are no lumps remaining and the batter is completely smooth.
4. Spoon the batter into the lined muffin cups, filling ¾ of the way. Place in preheated oven and bake for 18 – 22 minutes, until toothpick inserted in center comes out clean and they are golden on top.

Makes 12 muffins

Pancakes

The top tier in classic breakfast foods, pancakes are a universal wake-up call for kids on weekend mornings. It is quite difficult to find allergen-free pancakes in restaurants, so if you want to enjoy them it will likely be at home. The benefit of that is that you can customize them any way you like, be it with fruit, chocolate chips, cinnamon, or syrup.

This recipe does not call for any dairy, nuts, peanuts, citrus, or egg.

Tools You Will Need
Non-stick frying pan
Medium mixing bowl
Whisk
Measuring cups and spoons
Ladle
Spatula

Ingredients
2 cups all purpose flour
Pinch of salt
3 tsp baking powder
1 tsp baking soda
2 heaping tbsp confectioner's sugar
1 cup Coconut or Rice Dream
1 ½ cups water
¼ tsp pure vanilla extract
2 tbsp vegetable oil

Method
1. In a medium mixing bowl combine the flour, salt, baking powder, baking soda, and confectioner's sugar using a whisk.
2. Make a well in the center and add the coconut or rice milk, water, and pure vanilla extract and beat well. The batter will be a little bit lumpy.
3. If you want to add chopped bananas or blueberries this is the time do so! Toss blueberries in a bit of powdered sugar before adding to the batter to prevent them from sinking to the bottom of the batter.
4. Pour the oil in a non-stick frying pan and turn the heat to medium-high. Allow the pan to fully heat up before dropping in the batter or you will end up with tough, greasy pancakes (and no one wants that for breakfast!).
5. To test if the pan is hot enough, drop a tiny bit of batter into the oil and wait for it to start sizzling. When it sizzles it's ready for frying. Use a ladle to scoop the batter into the pan, making the pancakes relatively even in size. You can make dollar pancakes which only take about a minute on each side, or you can make large pancakes (about ½ cup batter at a time) which may take 2 – 3 minutes per side. The pancakes are ready to flip when the batter starts bubbling and the bubbles leave pockmarks on the surface. They should be nicely browned on the bottoms by this point.
6. Serve 'em while they're hot with maple syrup and fresh fruit.

Serves 4

Citrus and Poppy Seed Muffins

Light and airy muffins that are great on their own, with a glaze, or with icing. A good field trip snack for taking on the go!

Allergy Information

This recipe does not call for any dairy, nuts, peanuts, legumes.

Tools You Will Need

Muffin pan and liners

A medium mixing bowl

A fork or electric mixer

Measuring cups and spoons

A spoon

A knife and cutting board (if you plan to use fresh squeezed juice)

Ingredients

½ cup vegan margarine or shortening

1 cup sugar

¼ cup orange juice

½ cup water or rice milk

2 eggs

1 tsp vanilla

1 tsp baking soda

1 ½ tsp baking powder

A dash of salt

1 ½ cups flour

Juice of one lemon

Juice of one lime

1 tbsp poppy seeds

Method

1. Preheat your oven to 375F and line a muffin or mini loaf pan with paper liners.

2. Cream the vegan margarine or shortening cream and sugar with a fork or electric mixer until it is smooth. If you have trouble doing this by hand with a fork or if you are crunched for time, you should use the electric mixer.

3. Add the vanilla and eggs and beat well.

4. Slice the lemon and lime in half and squeeze the juices directly into your mixing bowl. Pour in the orange juice and water or rice milk. Beat the mixture very well so that everything is well combined.

5. Add the flour, baking powder, baking soda, and salt all at once and mix until everything is just combined.

6. Fold in the poppy seeds using a spoon.

7. Spoon the batter into your muffin or mini loaf pan, about ¾ of the way full, and place in your preheated oven.

8. Bake for 18 – 20 minutes, until a toothpick inserted in the center comes out clean.

9. Leave the muffins or mini loafs in the pan until they are cool enough to touch. Then transfer them to paper towels or a tea towel to cool completely.

10. If you want to glaze them, combine ½ cup of sugar with 2 tsp of water and mix until it is a thick paste. You can add ¼ tsp of water more at a time if the glaze is too dry. When the muffins are completely cooled you can dip the tops in this glaze and leave them on a rack or tray for at least an hour so that the glaze can firm up.

Makes 12 large cupcakes, or 16 – 18 medium cupcakes, or 30 – 38 mini cupcakes

Banana Bread Muffins

Ultra moist and packed with ripe banana flavor. This was one of the first recipes I mastered as a child, and remains one of my favorites today.

Allergen Information
This recipe does not call for any dairy, nuts, peanuts, citrus, or egg.

Tools You Will Need
Large mixing bowl
2 small mixing bowls
Large fork
Whisk
Mixing bowls and spoons
Muffin pan and paper muffin liners

Ingredients
1 $2/3$ cups flour
1 ½ tsp baking soda
2 tsp baking powder
Pinch of salt
½ cup shortening
½ cup sugar
¼ cup brown sugar
½ cup applesauce
1 ¼ cups mashed banana
½ tsp pure vanilla extract

Method
1. Preheat the oven to 350F.
2. Mash the banana in a small bowl until it's free of lumps. Add the applesauce and vanilla and mix well.
3. In another small bowl mix the flour, baking soda, baking powder, and salt. You can add 1 tbsp of cocoa powder or a sprinkle of cinnamon for extra flavor at this point for a more interesting and unusual flavor.
4. In a large mixing bowl cream the shortening and both sugars together until smooth.
5. Add the banana to the shortening mixture and mix well. Then begin folding the dry mixture in slowly until it is well combined and no lumps remain.
6. Line a muffin pan with paper liners. Scoop the batter into the cups so that they are ¾ full.
7. Bake for 30 minutes, or until the tops are golden brown and a toothpick inserted in the center comes out clean.

Zucchini Muffins

Zucchini is a great vegetable to add to baked goods because it keeps them so moist and tender without drastically altering the flavor. Young kids with discriminating palates will enjoy the sweet, mild taste of this bread. As a child this was one of my favorite recipes to make.

Allergen Information
This recipe does not call for any dairy, nuts, or peanuts.

Tools You Will Need
Large mixing bowl
Whisk
Grater
Measuring cups and spoons
Muffin pan
Paper muffin liners
Paring knife

Ingredients
1 ¾ cup grated zucchini
¼ cup sugar

1 cup brown sugar
1 tbsp molasses
2 eggs
½ tsp ground ginger
Juice of half a lemon
¾ cup vegetable oil
½ tsp vanilla
2 cups flour
1 tsp baking powder
½ tsp baking soda
Pinch of salt

Method
1. Preheat oven to 350F and line a muffin pan with paper liners.
2. Use a box grater, handheld grater, or food processor to grate the zucchini. Do not peel or remove the seeds, as they add wonderful texture and color to the batter. It is also best to grate the zucchini right before you start mixing the batter as it tends to let out a lot of moisture once it's grated, and preparing it ahead of time could leave you with a bowl of soggy zucchini to deal with.
3. Add the eggs, sugar, molasses, brown sugar, lemon juice, ginger, oil, and vanilla to the zucchini and beat well using a whisk.
4. Add the flour, baking powder, baking soda, and salt all at once and whisk until well combined but be careful not to over mix or it will alter the texture of the muffins.
5. Fill the muffin cups about ¾ of the way full with batter, then place the muffin pan in the oven and bake for 17 – 20 minutes. The muffins are done when a toothpick inserted in the center comes out clean and they are lightly golden on top.

Breakfast Muffins

Allergen information

This recipe does not call for any dairy, nuts, peanuts, legumes, or egg.

Tools You Will Need

A medium-sized mixing bowl

A fork or whisk

Measuring spoons and cups

Muffin pan (or a mini muffin pan)

Paper muffin cups

Ingredients

¾ cup vegetable oil

½ cup Rice Dream or Coconut Dream

1 cup of plain, unsweetened applesauce

1 tsp pure vanilla extract

Juice of half a lemon (any citrus will do)

1 ½ cups all purpose flour

½ cup sugar

1 ½ tsp baking soda

1 tsp baking powder

⅓ cup rolled oats

¼ cup quinoa "instant oats"

1 tsp ground cinnamon

½ tsp ground cardamom

2 tbsp organic honey

½ – ¾ cup fresh blueberries

⅓ cup peeled and diced apple

2 heaping tbsp Sunbutter

1 heaping tbsp molasses

Method

1. Preheat your oven to 375F.
2. Line muffin pan with paper muffin cups.
3. Add oil, water, Rice or Coconut Dream, applesauce, lemon juice, honey, Sunbutter, molasses, and pure vanilla extract to a medium mixing bowl. Combine well using a fork or whisk.
4. Add flour, sugar, baking soda, baking powder, oats, quinoa, cinnamon, and cardamom, to the wet ingredients all at once. Mix until just combined – make sure you do not over mix!
5. Add the blueberries and apple and fold together.
6. Spoon batter into lined muffin cups, about ¾ full.
7. Place in preheated 375F oven.
8. For medium cupcakes: bake for 18 – 22 minutes, until toothpick inserted in center comes out clean. For mini cupcakes: bake for 8 – 10 minutes, until toothpick inserted in center comes out clean.
9. Once removed from the oven, leave in the pan until they are cool enough to touch. Transfer to a paper towel, tea towel, or cooling rack, until they come to room temperature.

Makes 12 – 14 large muffins

Carrot Muffins

Allergen Information
This recipe does not call for any dairy, nuts, peanuts, or egg.

Tools You Will Need
Large mixing bowl
Whisk
Grater
Measuring cups and spoons
Muffin pan
Paper muffin liners
Paring knife

Ingredients

1 ¼ cups grated carrot
½ cup sugar
½ cup brown sugar
2 tbsp molasses
½ cup applesauce
Juice of half a navel orange
¾ cup vegetable oil

½ tsp pure vanilla extract
2 cups flour
1 tsp baking powder
1 ½ tsp baking soda
1 tsp ground cinnamon
Pinch of salt
A handful of raisins
½ cup drained cubed pineapple

Method

1. Preheat oven to 350F and line a muffin pan with paper liners.
2. Use a box grater, handheld grater, or food processor to grate the carrot. It is best to grate the carrot right before you start mixing the batter as it tends to dry out quite quickly.
3. Add the applesauce, sugar, brown sugar, orange juice, oil, molasses, and vanilla to the carrot and beat well using a whisk.
4. Add the flour, baking powder, baking soda, cinnamon, and salt all at once and whisk until well combined but be careful not to over mix or it will alter the texture of the muffins.
5. Add the raisins and cubed pineapple and fold it all together. You can chop up the pineapple chunks so that they are closer to the size of the raisins before adding to the batter.
6. Fill the muffin cups about ¾ of the way with batter, then place the muffin pan in the oven and bake for 18 – 20 minutes. The muffins are done when a toothpick inserted in the center comes out clean and they are lightly golden on top.

Makes 12 large muffins

POUND CAKE

It's always handy to have some signature desserts that you can store in your freezer and throw together at a moment's notice, especially because kids are known to be spontaneous decision makers at the best of times. My personal solution is to keep a loaf of pound cake in my freezer, as it can be so easily transformed into a variety of different desserts that will please both adults and kids alike.

Pound Cake

Pound cake is a staple recipe to have mastered for any aspiring baker. It can be eaten on its own or transformed into a number of delicious desserts such as trifles and marble cake. It freezes really well, meaning you can easily keep it on hand in case of a cake-craving emergency.

Allergen Information
This recipe does not call for any dairy, nuts, citrus, or peanuts.

Tools You Will Need
Large mixing bowl
Large whisk
Measuring cups and spoons
Parchment paper
Either 2 loaf pans or one slab cake pan

Ingredients
6 large eggs
1 ¾ cups sugar
¾ cup water
½ cup oil
2 ½ cups flour
2 heaping tsp baking powder

Method
1. Preheat oven to 350F.
2. In a large mixing bowl whisk together the eggs and sugar until smooth.
3. Add the water and oil and beat well.
4. Add the baking powder and one cup of the flour and beat until smooth.
5. Add the rest of the flour a half cup at a time, beating the batter until smooth each time.
6. Line your pan(s) with parchment paper and trim to size. Pour the batter into the pan(s) and smooth the top by gently wiggling the pan(s) back and forth on the counter.
7. Place in your preheated oven and bake for 1 hour (for loaf pans) or 35 – 45 minutes (for slab pan). The cake is finished baking when it is golden on top and a toothpick inserted in the center comes out clean. Allow to cool fully before transferring to a plate.

*Tip: This cake freezes really well! Store in a freezer strength plastic zipper bag and allow to defrost on the counter either the night before or the morning of the day you intend to use it.

Pound Cake Trifle

One of the simplest ways to transform a basic pound cake into an impressive dessert is to make a trifle. A trifle is the layering of cake, fruit, and something creamy to bind it together in a glass or serving dish. This particular recipe is for individual servings of trifle. I recommend you serve them in a pretty mug or glass so that your guests can see the layers of filling they are about to enjoy.

Tools You Will Need
2 mugs or cups, preferably clear
Spoon
Knife

Ingredients
Strawberry Jam (found on page 249)
Coconut Cream Drizzle (found on page 247)
A chunk of leftover pound cake (found on page 47) about 4" x 4"
A handful of blueberries (or the berry of your choice)

Method
This is a very loose recipe to follow and you can in fact make substitutions anywhere you like. None of the measurements are precise, and you can really change it up to suit your tastes.

1. Use the mouth of your glass or cup to cut out a thick section of leftover pound cake.
2. Stand the piece on its side and use a paring knife to slice it into 4 round sections. They can be as thin or thick as you like; I would suggest 1 cm thickness.
3. Line the bottom of each glass or mug with blueberries and then add a dollop of coconut cream drizzle on top.
4. Then layer in a slice of pound cake and top it with a generous scoop of strawberry jam and some more coconut cream drizzle. You can add more blueberries if you like as well.
5. Place another piece of pound cake on top and layer on more strawberry jam and coconut cream drizzle. Top it off artfully with a few blueberries and some fresh mint if you have any. You can also add a drizzle of honey, some orange zest, or a sprinkling of cinnamon.
6. Refrigerate for an hour to let all the flavors soak into the cake before devouring.

Serves 2

Pound Cake French Toast

It's a shame to throw away day old pound cake that's gone a bit stale, or to throw out weeks old pound cake that has been left in the freezer. A great way to make use of stale pound cake is to make it into French toast. By soaking the cake in a light and flavorful batter it regains its richness and moist texture. Frying it quickly in oil forms just the right amount of crispy goodness on the outside. I think this recipe is a great substitute for traditional French Toast made with bread because it can be really difficult to find breads that are allergen-free. This recipe is well served for breakfast or dessert.

Allergen Information
This recipe does not call for any dairy, nuts, citrus, or peanuts.

Tools You Will Need
Medium mixing bowl
Whisk
Non-stick frying pan
Spatula

Ingredients
2 tbsp vegetable oil
2 large eggs
½ tsp cinnamon
A pinch of cardamom (optional)
1 tbsp coconut milk fat (found in canned coconut milk)
½ cup Rice Dream
1 tsp pure vanilla extract
2 tbsp sugar
10 – 12 thick (½ inch) slices of pound cake (found on page 47)
Berries and maple syrup for dressing

Method
1. Use a whisk to beat the egg, cinnamon, cardamom, coconut milk fat, Rice Dream, vanilla, and sugar until well combined. The measurements in this recipe are very loose; if you prefer more or less cinnamon or sugar, for example, you can adjust the measurements to suit your liking.
2. Heat the oil in a non-stick frying pan. Drop a dab of the batter in the pan to test if it's hot enough, and when the batter begins to sizzle the pan is ready for the French toast. Dunk each slice of pound cake into the batter right before dropping it into the hot pan. Make sure it's well coated in batter on all sides. The texture may seem a little soggy but don't worry, that's normal. Fry about 4 or 5 slices at a time, making sure not to overcrowd the pan. Allow to fry on medium-high heat for about 5 minutes on each side. Check that the bottoms are browned before flipping.
3. Serve with fresh berries, applesauce, or maple syrup.

Serves 3 – 4

Vanilla Cake Balls

Cake pops are a very strong trend right now. There are a lot of gadgets and kits out there to help you bake the perfect cake pop, but personally I prefer the homemade-looking variety. And rolling the cake balls by hand can be a lot of fun! If you're feeling adventurous or just want to mix it up, try changing the recipe to chocolate.

Allergen Information
This recipe does not call for any dairy, nuts, citrus, or peanuts.

Tools You Will Need
Large mixing bowl
Spatula
Electric mixer
Paring knife
Parchment paper
Baking sheet
Small mixing bowl
Measuring cups
Spoon

Ingredients
½ cup vegan butter or shortening
2 – 3 drops red food coloring
½ tsp pure vanilla extract
1 ½ cups confectioner's sugar
2 ½ cups crumbled pound cake (found on page 47)
Sprinkles or coconut for dipping

Method
1. Cream together the vanilla, food coloring, and vegan butter or shortening using an electric mixer on medium speed until smooth.
2. Begin adding the confectioner's sugar a half cup at a time, beating in the Rice Dream a half tbsp at a time in between additions.
3. Use a paring knife to trim the bottom and side crusts off the cake. Because the crusts are a darker color than the spongy inside, they will not blend in well with the rest of the batter and will give it a sort of dirty appearance. Use your fingers to crumble the cake directly into the frosting. Try to crumble it as fine as possible and avoid large chunks.
4. Use a spatula to fold the cake crumbs into the frosting so that it is all well combined and uniformly pink in color.
5. Use a small spoon to scoop out quarter-sized portions of batter and roll each one into a ball in your hand. Set them out on a baking sheet lined with parchment paper to prevent sticking.
6. Pour coconut or sprinkles into a small bowl. Roll each cake ball around in the topping so that all sides are well coated. Return them to the parchment lined baking sheet and refrigerate for an hour to allow them to firm up before serving.

Makes 20 – 25 cake balls

Cake Skewers

Let's face it, not all kids are fans of frothy frosting. For those who prefer the actual cake to the frosting that adorns it, there is the cake skewer. Kind of like a shish kebab, cake skewers are layers of cake, fruit, and marshmallows dipped in melted chocolate on a bamboo skewer. Simply layering cake and fruit on the skewer is a great opportunity to get really little hands involved in the kitchen too! This recipe can be scaled up and done like a craft activity at a birthday party so that everyone can customize their own cool cake-kebab.

Allergen Information

This recipe does not call for any dairy, nuts, citrus, or peanuts.

Tools You Will Need

10 Bamboo skewers

1.5 – 2 inch diameter cookie cutters (simple shapes are preferable)

Paring knife

Double boiler (small saucepan, medium metal mixing bowl, spatula)

Parchment paper

Baking sheet

Ingredients

half of 1 Pound Cake (found on page 47)

1 lb strawberries

1 pint blueberries

half of a whole peeled and cored pineapple

1 bag of large marshmallows

1 cup melted Enjoy Life chocolate chips

Sprinkles

Method

1. Line the baking sheet with parchment paper. Use the blunt end of each bamboo skewer to pierce a marshmallow, but don't fully pierce the marshmallow through. Although marshmallows and sprinkles are generally dairy- and nut-free, be sure to read the ingredients before purchasing to ensure they are safe. Use the skewer like a fork to dip the top of each marshmallow into the melted chocolate and then place on the parchment-lined baking sheet. Dust the chocolate covered areas with sprinkles. Refrigerate for an hour so that the chocolate has set enough not to smear or drip while loading the rest of the components onto the skewer.

The chocolate chips can be melted using a double boiler. Fill a saucepan with water to a depth of 1 inch. Turn the stove to medium-low heat and place the metal mixing bowl on top. Pour the chocolate chips in the bowl and begin to slowly stir them using a spatula once the edges of the chips start to melt. Continue to stir until the chocolate is completely melted and then immediately remove the bowl from on top of the saucepan and turn off the heat to prevent burning.

2. Cut the crusts off 1/2 lb. of pound cake and cut into 1 inch thick slices. Use cookie cutters to cut fun shapes out of the cake slices. Simple shapes like hearts, stars, and flowers really work best for this because small or ornate edges will easily crumble off. Set the cake shapes aside.

3. Wash the fruit and remove any stems, leaves, or core. The pineapple can be cut into 1/2 inch cubes or sliced and then cut out with cookie cutters. Set the fruit aside.

4. When the chocolate covered marshmallows have set after an hour, remove the skewers from the fridge. Slide 1 each of the fruits and cake shapes onto each skewer in whatever order you like. There's no right or wrong way to do this! Each skewer can look different, or they can all look the same. You can also replace any of the fruits with ones that are local to your area, in season, or just happen to be your favorites. You can also drizzle melted chocolate on the fruit and cake shapes once they are on the skewers. Refrigerate the skewers until ready to serve.

Serves 10

"Bread" Pudding

Pound cake is the chameleon of cakes, and can easily be substituted for actual bread to make bread pudding. This pudding is slow baked with berries and a creamy batter to make it moist and delicious. I suggest you serve it with tea and berries.

Allergen Information
This recipe does not call for any dairy, nuts, or peanuts.

Tools You Will Need
Medium mixing bowl
Square glass baking dish
Whisk
Aluminum foil
Measuring cups and spoons

Ingredients
¾ cup Rice Dream
2 large eggs
½ of a leftover pound cake
1 tsp pure vanilla extract
Pinch of salt
Several handfuls of blueberries
⅓ cup Coconut Dream
1 tsp orange zest
Several pads of Earth Balance

Method
1. Preheat oven to 350F.
2. Slice about ¼ of a batch of leftover pound cake into ½ inch thick slices and stagger them around your baking dish so that the corners are sort of poking up (see photo). There is no right or wrong way to do this, but you should avoid stacking the slices because the batter will not be able to penetrate the cake properly if there are no gaps.
3. In a medium mixing bowl combine the Rice Dream, eggs, vanilla, salt, orange zest, and Coconut Dream. Whisk well, until everything is well combined and there are no globs of egg white remaining.
4. Pour the mixture over the pound cake, making sure to distribute it evenly and into all corners. The cake should be well soaked. At this point don't be shy to get in there with your fingers and move pieces of cake around in the pan to not only make it look prettier but also to help distribute the liquid.
5. Toss the berries on top of the soaked pound cake, again making sure to evenly disperse them around the whole pan.
6. You can add a few little pads of Earth Balance on top of the pudding to add a bit of richness, but this is entirely optional and your dessert will not suffer if you opt out of this step.
7. Cover the pan with aluminum foil and place in preheated oven for 15 minutes, then remove the cover and bake for an additional 15 – 20 minutes, until the edges of the cake are golden brown. This pudding is best served warm, and in my opinion, for breakfast.

Marble Coffee Cake

One need not be a coffee drinker to appreciate a good coffee cake. Kids will love it for its mellow vanilla taste and the swirl of chocolate that runs through the center. Parents will love it for the same reasons and, obviously, because it goes so well with a morning coffee.

Allergen Information

This recipe does not call for any dairy, nuts, citrus, or peanuts.

Tools You Will Need

Large mixing bowl

Small mixing bowl

Whisk

Measuring cups and spoons

Parchment paper

8 inch square or round cake pan

Knife or toothpick

Ingredients

3 large eggs

¾ cup sugar

$^1/_3$ cup water

¼ cup oil

1 tsp pure vanilla extract

1 ¼ cups flour

1 tsp ground cinnamon

1 heaping tsp baking powder

1 heaping tbsp cocoa powder

Method

1. Preheat oven to 350F.

2. In a large mixing bowl whisk together the eggs and sugar until smooth.

3. Add the water, vanilla and oil and beat well.

4. Add the baking powder, cinnamon, and flour and beat until smooth.

5. Remove ½ cup of batter and pour into a small mixing bowl. Add the cocoa to the small bowl of batter and beat well. Set aside.

6. Line your pan with parchment paper and trim to size. Pour the main bowl of batter into the pan and smooth the top by gently wiggling the pan back and forth on the counter.

7. Use a small spoon to scoop out about ¼ of the chocolate batter and drop it into the vanilla batter in a straight line. Proceed to do this 3 more times so that all the chocolate batter has been used up and your vanilla cake has 4 lines of chocolate batter running through it. Then take either a knife or toothpick and drag it through the batter in the opposite direction the chocolate lines are running. Do this 3 or 4 more times so that the chocolate and vanilla are well marbled together. You can play around with the directions you use, and can also try making a swirl pattern for something a little different.

8. Place the baking dish in preheated oven and bake for 1 hour 25 – 30 minutes. The cake is finished baking when it is golden on top and a toothpick inserted in the center comes out clean. Allow to cool fully before transferring to a plate.

*Tip: This cake freezes really well! Store in a freezer strength plastic zipper bag and allow to defrost on the counter either the night before or the morning of the day you intend to use it.

Decadent Chocolate Pound Cake

Allergen Information
This recipe does not call for any dairy, nuts, peanuts, or citrus.

Tools You Will Need
Large mixing bowl
Whisk
Measuring cups and spoons
Loaf pan or 8 inch round cake pan
Parchment paper
Oven mitts

Ingredients
¼ cup oil
3 large eggs
1 cup sugar
½ cup water
1 cup flour
¼ cup cocoa
1 heaping tsp baking powder
A pinch of salt
1 tsp pure vanilla extract

Method
1. Preheat oven to 350F.
2. In a large mixing bowl whisk together the eggs and sugar until smooth.
3. Add the water, oil, and vanilla and beat well.
4. Add the baking powder, salt, and half of the cup of the flour and beat until smooth.
5. Add the rest of the flour and cocoa a quarter cup at a time, beating the batter until smooth each time.
6. Line your pan(s) with parchment paper and trim to size. Pour the batter into the pan(s) and smooth the top by gently wiggling the pan(s) back and forth on the counter.
7. Place in your preheated oven and bake for 1 hour (for loaf pans) or 35 – 45 minutes (for slab pan). The cake is finished baking when it is golden on top and a toothpick inserted in the center comes out clean. Allow to cool fully before transferring to a plate.

Macaroons

A classic quick dessert that highlights the creamy flavor of coconut, finessed with a touch of pink.

Allergen Information
This recipe does not call for any dairy, nuts, citrus, or peanuts.

Tools You Will Need
Large mixing bowl
Whisk
Spatula or mixing spoon
Parchment paper
Measuring cups and spoons
Baking sheet
Cookie scoop or small ice cream scoop

Ingredients
½ tsp pure vanilla extract
2 egg whites
3 ⅓ cups Let's Do Organic shredded coconut
½ cup confectioner's sugar
Pinch of salt
2 drops red food coloring

Method
1. Preheat the oven to 325F and line a baking sheet with parchment paper.
2. In a large bowl beat the egg whites, sugar, vanilla, and red food coloring together using a whisk. You don't have to beat till the egg whites form peaks. Just beat enough that they form a bit of froth.
3. Add the coconut and use a spatula or spoon to fold it all together.
4. Use a cookie scoop or small ice cream scoop to give the macaroons a nice round shape when transferring to the baking sheet. Space them 1 inch apart. If you don't have one on hand you can always use a regular spoon to drop them onto the pan. Just be sure to use your hands to form them afterwards so that they are sticking together enough to keep their shape. If the macaroon is too loose it will easily crumble apart.
5. Place the baking sheet in preheated oven and bake for 18 – 20 minutes, until they've formed a golden shell. Allow to cool completely before transferring to a plate.

Makes 15 – 18 macaroons

Spicy Shortbread Cookies

For the more adventurous beginner foodie, these shortbread cookies have a hint of spice and crunch that gives them a unique flavor. Flaked red chilies and cornmeal mean they go well with a bowl of soup or simply as a snack on their own.

Allergen Information
This recipe does not call for any dairy, nuts, citrus, or peanuts.

Tools You Will Need
Measuring cups and spoons
Medium mixing bowl
Parchment paper
Baking sheet
Fork or electric mixer

Ingredients
1 cup vegan butter
²/₃ cup sugar
¼ tsp salt
1 egg
1 ¾ cups flour
1 tsp baking powder
1 tbsp hot chili flakes
5 tbsp cornmeal

Method
1. Preheat oven to 375F.
2. In a medium mixing bowl cream the vegan butter or shortening and sugar until smooth. You can do this with a fork or an electric mixer on medium speed.
3. Add the salt, chili flakes, and egg and beat until smooth.
4. Fold in the flour and baking powder all at once, mixing until no clumps remain.
5. Pour the cornmeal into a small bowl and set aside.
6. Scoop out loonie sized amounts of dough and roll them into a ball in your hand. Roll each ball of dough in cornmeal so that they are fully coated. It's okay if there is excess cornmeal stuck to the outside.
7. Place the balls of dough on a baking sheet about 1 inch apart and lightly squish each one down with the heel of your hand.
8. Place in your preheated oven and bake for 7 – 9 minutes, until lightly golden on the edges.

Makes 20 – 25 cookies

Maple Molasses Sandwich Cookies

The all-Canadian dessert: two maple-infused sugar cookies are stuffed with a rich frosting flavored by molasses and maple syrup. They go perfectly with a cup of tea in a snowstorm.

Allergen Information

This recipe does not call for any dairy, nuts, citrus, or peanuts.

Tools You Will Need

Large mixing bowl
Large fork or electric mixer
Measuring cups and spoons
Baking sheet
Oven mitts

Ingredients

Cookie
1 cup vegan butter or shortening
½ cup sugar
4 heaping tbsp demerara or dark
    brown sugar
1 tbsp maple syrup
2 tbsp molasses
A pinch of salt
2 eggs

1 tsp vanilla
2 ¼ cups flour
1 tsp baking powder
½ tsp baking soda

Filling
½ cup vegan butter or shortening
¼ cup maple syrup
2 tbsp molasses
2 cups confectioner's sugar

Method

1. Preheat oven to 375F.

2. In a large bowl cream the sugars, vegan butter or shortening, maple syrup, and molasses together using either a fork or an electric mixer on medium speed. Mix until smooth and well combined.

3. Add the vanilla and eggs and mix well.

4. Add half of the flour and mix until just combined. Then add the rest of the flour, baking soda, baking powder, and salt and mix well. It should come together in a loose, sticky dough.

5. Use a small spoon to scoop quarter-sized amounts into your palm and roll into a ball. Drop the balls on a baking sheet and squish down with the heel of your hand, trying to keep them all relatively the same shape and size. Space the cookies about ½ inch apart as they will rise while baking.

6. Place in preheated oven and bake for 7 – 9 minutes for chewy, or 9 – 11 minutes for crunchy cookies.

7. While the cookies are baking you can prepare the filling. Use a fork to mash together the vegan butter or shortening, maple syrup, and molasses until it's smooth and silky.

8. Add the confectioner's sugar a half cup at a time, mixing until creamy after each addition.

9. Allow the cookies to cool on a rack before filling. Try to match the cookies up so that they are each paired with one of roughly the same shape and size. These cookies are supposed to look a little rustic so don't worry if they don't match up perfectly.

10. Place a dollop of filling onto the underside of half the cookies, and then place their matching cookies on top and press lightly to disperse the filling inside.

11. They can be eaten immediately, or refrigerated for a half hour to allow the filling to firm up again.

Makes 30 – 35 cookies

Fudgy Sandwich Cookies

Creamy chocolate sandwiched between crunchy chocolate cookies. A guaranteed hit with any crowd.

Allergen Information

This recipe does not call for any dairy, nuts, citrus, or peanuts.

Tools You Will Need

Large mixing bowl

Electric mixer or a fork

Measuring cups and spoons

Small spoon

Baking sheet

Small saucepan

Medium metal mixing bowl

Spatula

Ingredients

Cookie

1 cup vegan butter or shortening

½ cup sugar

1 heaping tbsp demerara or dark brown sugar

A pinch of salt

1 egg

1 tsp vanilla

1 ¼ cups flour

$^1/_3$ cup cocoa powder

1 tsp baking powder

½ tsp baking soda

Filling

$^1/_3$ cup vegan butter or shortening

$^1/_3$ cup Enjoy Life chocolate chips

1 tbsp cocoa powder

Method

1. Preheat oven to 375F.

2. In a large mixing bowl cream the vegan butter or shortening, sugar, and brown sugar until smooth. If using an electric mixer, set to medium speed.

3. Add the egg and vanilla and mix until well combined.

4. In a separate bowl combine the flour, cocoa, baking powder, baking soda, and salt. Add it about ¾ cup at a time to the wet ingredients, stirring well after each addition.

5. Use a small spoon to scoop out quarter-sized portions of dough. Roll each scoop of dough into a ball in the palm of your hand and then place on a baking sheet and lightly squish down with the heel of your hand. Place each cookie ½ inch apart.

6. Place in a preheated oven and bake for 5 – 7 minutes, depending on how soft or crunchy you prefer them. After baking allow to cool completely before adding the filling.

7. To make the filling, fill a small saucepan with water about 1 inch deep. Place a medium-sized metal mixing bowl on top and turn the heat to medium-low to create a double boiler.

8. Add the chocolate and vegan butter or shortening to the bowl and begin to slowly stir it with a spatula until it is completely melted and smooth. As soon as all the chocolate is melted turn the heat off and remove the bowl from on top of the pot. Add the cocoa powder (you may want to sift it if it is lumpy) and mix well.

9. Scoop a dollop of chocolate filling onto the bottoms of half the batch of cooled cookies. Then place another cookie on top to create a sandwich.

10. Refrigerate for a half hour to allow the chocolate to set before serving.

Makes 20 – 25 sandwich cookies

Swirl Cookies

These sugar cookies may look like they took a lot of effort, time, and precision, but they are actually really simple to create. Once you become more confident at handling the dough you can incorporate more layers and colors into the swirl to really impress.

Allergen Information

This recipe does not call for any dairy, nuts, citrus, or peanuts.

Tools You Will Need

Large mixing bowl
Fork
Rolling pin

Measuring cups and spoons
Parchment paper
Cookie cutter(s)
Baking sheet

Ingredients

1 cup vegan butter or shortening
1 cup sugar
Pinch of salt
1 egg
1 tsp vanilla
1 ¾ cups flour
1 tsp baking powder
8 drops of any 1 food color

Method

1. In a large mixing bowl mash the vegan butter or shortening together with the sugar using a fork. Mash until it is creamy in texture.
2. Add the egg and vanilla and beat well.
3. Add the flour and baking powder and mix well. The dough should come together in a rough clump at this point. You can stop mixing when all the dry ingredients are absorbed and the dough has come together in a ball.
4. Line your counter with a piece of parchment paper. Dump the dough out onto the parchment paper and use your hands to press it together into a square disk. Cut it in half and put one half back into the mixing bowl.
5. Add the food color to the dough and use a fork or spoon to mix until it is uniformly one color. Place the dough back on the parchment, and shape it into a square disk. Wrap the parchment around the dough and leave it to chill in the fridge for at least 2 hours.
6. When it's finished chilling, unwrap the parchment paper and separate the two colors of dough. Press the white one out into a rough square about 5 x 5 inches. Then place the colored one on top and press it out to the same shape. Make sure the dough is in the center of the parchment paper.
7. Dust the dough in confectioner's sugar to prevent it from sticking to the rolling pin. You can dust the rolling pin with confectioner's sugar as well. Preheat the oven to 375F.
8. Roll the dough out to ¼ inch thickness, making sure to have a light touch so that the colored layer stays uniformly on top of the white layer.
9. When the dough is rolled out, lift one edge on the lengthwise side and begin to roll it. You can slowly lift the parchment paper as you go along to help you roll it into a long log. It's important that the dough is rolled out nice and thin because the thicker the dough is, the wider the cookies will be. When it's fully rolled into a log you can use your hands to shape it more evenly.
10. Use a non-serrated knife to slice the log into ½ inch thick discs. Place the cookies on a baking sheet, spaced about 1 inch apart.
11. Place the baking sheet in preheated oven and bake for 6 – 8 minutes, until lightly golden on top.

Makes 20 – 25 cookies

Salted Honey and Mint Sugar Cookies

These soft baked sugar cookies are laden with fresh mint and sweet honey swirled throughout. The salt goes almost undetected except that it adds a bit of extra flavor and really amplifies the taste of the honey. These are great when dunked in tea and freeze well.

Allergen Information
This recipe does not call for any dairy, nuts, citrus, or peanuts.

Tools You Will Need
Medium mixing bowl
Fork
Measuring cups and spoons
Baking sheet

Ingredients
¾ cup Earth Balance
¾ cup white sugar
½ tsp pure vanilla extract
4 tbsp organic honey
A pinch of salt
1 large egg
1 cup all purpose flour
½ tsp baking powder
¼ tsp baking soda
10 fresh mint leaves

Method
1. Preheat oven to 375F.
2. Use a fork to cream the Earth Balance and sugar together until smooth and fluffy. Then add half the honey and mix well, reserving 2 tbsp of honey for later.
3. Add the vanilla and egg and continue to beat well with a fork.
4. Add the salt and half the flour and fold into the wet ingredients using a fork.
5. Then add the remaining flour, baking soda, and baking powder and mix well but be sure not to over mix. It should come together into a moist dough.
6. Wash and pat dry the mint leaves to remove any excess water which could ruin the texture of the cookie dough. Break the leaves into small pieces using your fingers. The pieces don't have to be uniform or pretty, they just have to be small. Fold them into the cookie batter.
7. Drizzle the remaining honey over the batter and give it a rough mix, leaving little pockets of honey throughout. This adds a slight marble finish to the baked cookies and gives a subtle hint that they contain honey.
8. Use a spoon to scoop out dollops of dough about the size of a half-dollar and roll each one into a ball in your hand. Then set them 2 inches apart on a baking sheet and squish down with the heel of your hand.
9. Place in preheated oven and bake for 7 – 9 minutes, until the edges are golden brown. For a crispy cookie bake for 9 – 11 minutes.

Makes 20 cookies

Sunbutter Cookies

Allergic kids know what it's like to grow up being told they are so unlucky to not be able to try peanut butter cookies or any peanut butter related product. Luckily we now have a substitute called Sunbutter that I am told tastes exactly like real peanut butter (though I'll never be able to confirm that for myself). Sunbutter cookies are one of my go-to quick recipes because they create very little mess and only use a few ingredients to make a delicious cookie. I also really like the fact that they are gluten-free and pack a punch of protein.

Allergen Information
This recipe does not call for any dairy, nuts, peanuts, citrus, or gluten.

Tools You Will Need
Measuring cup
Medium mixing bowl
Fork
Baking sheet
Spoon

Ingredients
¼ cup sugar
¼ cup brown sugar
1 cup Sunbutter (organic unsweetened works best)
1 large egg
A pinch of salt
$1/3$ cup Enjoy Life chocolate mini chips

Method
1. Preheat oven to 375F.
2. Using a fork mix all the ingredients together until smooth.
3. Use a spoon to scoop out dollops of dough about the size of a half-dollar and roll each one into a ball in your hand.
4. Place the cookies 2 inches apart on a baking sheet and squish down with the heel of your hand. You can use a fork to make a criss-cross pattern on top like a typical peanut butter cookie if you choose.
5. Place in preheated oven and bake for 8 – 10 minutes.
6. Allow the cookies to cool on the baking sheet for 10 minutes after baking so that they can firm up enough to transfer to a plate or cooling rack.

Makes 20 cookies

Fig and Raisin Cookies

This recipe is for kids who love the sweet richness of dried fruits. Having an Italian dad, we always had dried figs in the cupboard at my house which I really loved. They go so well with the taste of honey and oats. I created this recipe when I was a teenager to please my dad who always requested dried fruits in his cookies instead of the chocolate chips I usually used to please my brother. This recipe became a winner all around and I have continued to make it for years. I hope your family enjoys it too.

Allergen Information
This recipe does not call for any dairy, nuts, citrus, or peanuts.

Tools You Will Need	Ingredients	
Small bowl	3 dried figs	½ cup sugar
Chopping knife	⅓ cup raisins	⅓ cup brown sugar
Large mixing bowl	2 tsp pure vanilla extract	1 tsp organic honey
Mixing spoon or spatula	½ cup water	1 egg
Baking sheet	1 cup flour	2 tbsp Rice Dream
Measuring cups and spoons	½ tsp baking powder	1 cup instant oats or quinoa instant
Small strainer	½ tsp baking soda	"oats"
Paper towels	½ cup Earth Balance or shortening	

Method
1. Preheat oven to 375F.
2. Soak the raisins in a small bowl with the water and pure vanilla extract about 15 minutes before you start creating the cookie dough. This will cause them to plump up and be a lot juicier after baking.
3. Remove the stems from 3 dried figs. Chop the figs up as fine as possible and set aside.
4. In a large mixing bowl combine the Earth Balance or shortening and sugars by mashing with a fork until smooth.
5. Add the honey, egg, and Rice Dream and mix until well combined.
6. Add the flour, baking powder, and baking soda, and mix well but be careful not to over mix or the dough will become too tough.
7. Drain the raisins in a small strainer and pat dry with paper towels. Add them to the dough along with the chopped figs and instant oats. Fold into the dough using a fork until all the ingredients are evenly dispersed.
8. Scoop out dollops of dough about the size of a quarter using a spoon and drop them onto a baking sheet 2 inches apart. Since these are a basic drop cookie you don't need to form them into discs before baking; however, you can do so if you prefer a batch of more uniform cookies.
9. Place the baking sheet in a preheated oven and bake for 8 – 10 minutes, until golden brown.

Makes 25 – 35 cookies

Crunchy Sandwich Cookies

Fresh jam sandwiched between 2 crispy and light cookies. This recipe is a great way to sneak real fruit and quinoa into snack time.

Allergy Information
This recipe does not call for any dairy, nuts, peanuts, gluten, or citrus.

Tools You Will Need
Measuring cups and spoons
Medium size mixing bowl
A fork
Parchment paper
2 baking sheets
Medium size saucepan
A small bowl
A spoon
Cutting board and knife

Ingredients
¼ cup vegan butter or shortening
½ cup sugar
¼ cup brown sugar
1 tsp vanilla
1 egg
¼ cup unsweetened shredded coconut flakes
¾ tsp baking soda
1 ¼ cups sifted quinoa flour
½ pint of raspberries
1 pint of strawberries
3 tbsp confectioner's sugar

Method

Strawberry-Raspberry Filling
If you are in a rush you can use store bought jam. But if you have the time, it is worth it to make it from scratch!

1. Wash the strawberries and raspberries. Cut the strawberries into quarters.
2. Put them in a medium - saucepan and add the confectioner's sugar. Stir it all up so all the berries are coated in confectioner's sugar.
3. Turn the heat to medium-low and bring the berries to a simmer. **Simmering** means that bubbles are starting to come up to the surface, but not as many or as quickly as **boiling**. Boiling brings the berries up to a higher temperature. Be careful, because you do not want the berries to burn!
4. Once they are simmering, turn the heat down to low. Leave them on low, uncovered, for about 15 – 20 minutes, stirring often. They will become very smooth, soft, and silky looking.
5. Pour the mixture into a bowl and put it in the fridge for at least an hour and a half. You can even put it in overnight. The berries will become very firm, like a jam.

Wafers

1. Preheat the oven to 375F and line the baking sheet with parchment paper.
2. Mash the vegan butter or shortening with a fork until it is smooth. Then add the sugar and brown sugar and beat together with a fork until the mixture is fluffy.
3. Add the vanilla and egg and beat until the mixture is smooth.
4. Then add the coconut, baking soda, and quinoa flour all at once. Mix well.
5. Scoop batter out about one tbsp at a time, and form into balls. Place them at least an inch apart on the baking sheet and slightly flatten the tops. They will flatten a lot more when they bake.
6. Place the tray in a preheated oven and bake for 8 minutes. When they are done they will be very soft. Let them sit on the baking sheet until they have cooled completely, and then move them to a serving plate. They will have become very firm.

Assembling the sandwiches

1. The sandwiches are ready to make when the jam and the wafers are completely cooled. Scoop about 1 to 2 tsp of jam onto the flat bottom of a wafer. Then sandwich it with another wafer on top. Don't squeeze or press them too hard, or the jam will squish out!
2. You can dust them with confectioner's sugar for extra sparkle!

Makes 24 wafer cookies, or 12 sandwich cookies

Shaped Sugar Cookies

When in doubt, make sugar cookies. They are guaranteed to please and are so simple to create. Kids will love decorating and cutting them into fun shapes.

This recipe does not call for any dairy, nuts, citrus, or peanuts.

Tools You Will Need
Measuring cups and spoons
Medium mixing bowl
Large fork
Parchment paper
Rolling pin
Cookie cutters

Ingredients
2 cups flour
²/₃ cup shortening
Pinch of salt
½ tsp baking powder
1 egg
¾ cup sugar
5 – 8 drops food coloring

Method
1. Preheat the oven to 375F.
2. In a large mixing bowl cream the shortening, sugar, and salt together using a large fork.
3. Add the food coloring and egg and beat well.
4. Fold in the flour all at once and mix until well combined. It will come together as a lump of dough.
5. Tear off a piece of parchment paper large enough to roll the dough out on afterwards. Place the dough in the center and wrap the parchment paper around it, then refrigerate for 2 hours. This will allow it to firm up enough to roll out without sticking.
6. Once the dough has rested remove it from the fridge. Leaving it on the parchment paper, lightly dust with flour on all sides. Lightly dust the rolling pin as well and then roll the dough out to ½ inch thickness. You'll have to work quite quickly, as the dough becomes stickier as it warms up.
7. Lightly dust your desired cookie cutter(s) and begin cutting out shapes, placing them ½ inch apart on a baking sheet.
8. Place in the oven for 5 – 8 minutes, depending on the size of the shapes you made. You can sprinkle some sugar or cinnamon (or both) over the cookies before baking. While the first batch is in the oven be sure to wrap up the remaining dough and refrigerate to allow it to firm up again.

Makes 25 – 35 cookies depending on the size of your cookie cutter

Red Velvet Sugar Cookies

Red velvet is the name given to chocolate flavored cakes and cookies that are dyed red. The rich chocolatey taste is almost a shock for those fooled by the deep red color.

Allergen Information
This recipe does not call for any dairy, nuts, citrus, or peanuts.

Tools You Will Need
Large mixing bowl
Measuring cups and spoons
Large fork
Parchment paper
Rolling pin
Round cookie cutter
Electric mixer
Spoon
Pastry bag with tip (optional)

Ingredients
1 ²/₃ cups flour
¹/₃ cup cocoa powder
²/₃ cup shortening
Pinch of salt
½ tsp baking powder
1 egg
¾ cup sugar
10 ml red food coloring

Filling
½ cup shortening
1 ½ cups confectioner's sugar
½ tsp vanilla
1 tbsp honey
2 tsp water

*In a pinch you can always leave the wafers unfilled or roll the dough out to ¼ inch thickness and fill them with honey and cinnamon or marshmallow fluff after baking. It is relatively easy to find allergen-free marshmallow fluff.

Method

1. In a large mixing bowl cream the shortening, salt, and sugar using a large fork until smooth.

2. Add the egg and food coloring and beat well, until the whole mixture has turned light pink.

3. Add the flour, cocoa powder, and baking powder all at once and mix until there are no cocoa lumps remaining and the dough comes together in a ball.

4. Turn the dough onto a large piece of parchment paper that would be large enough to roll it out on. Wrap it up and refrigerate for 2 hours to allow the dough to firm up.

5. To make the filling, cream the shortening, vanilla, and honey in a mixing bowl using an electric mixer until smooth. Add the sugar slowly, about a half cup at a time with the mixer on medium speed to prevent spraying powdered sugar all around your kitchen.

6. Add the water 1 tsp at a time if the frosting begins to thicken up too much. The filling should be quite thick, but still smooth enough to spread easily with a spoon. Set aside at room temperature until the wafers are ready to fill.

7. Preheat the oven to 375F.

8. When the dough is finished chilling, unwrap the parchment paper and lightly dust with some extra confectioner's sugar on all sides, and dust the rolling pin as well to prevent sticking.

9. Roll the dough out to ¼ inch thickness, then cut into circles using either a cookie cutter or the mouth of a glass and place on a baking sheet ½ inch apart.

10. Bake for 5 – 8 minutes depending on whether you prefer your cookies soft or crunchy.

11. Allow them to cool completely on a cooling rack before filling to prevent the frosting from melting.

12. You can fill the cookies using a pastry bag to make a nice even swirl in the middle, or you can simply spoon a dollop of frosting onto one cookie and sandwich it with another. For chocolate filling, replace ¼ cup of confectioner's sugar with ¼ cup sifted cocoa powder. Adding some freshly grated orange zest to the filling is also a lovely complement to the taste of red velvet.

Makes approximately. 15 sandwich cookies

Chocolate Chip Cookies

No matter how many others he tried, chocolate chip cookies will always be my brother's cookie of choice. Over the years I must have made hundreds of batches of them, so it's safe to say that this recipe is one I've got down to a T.

Allergen Information

This recipe does not call for any dairy, nuts, citrus, or peanuts.

Tools You Will Need

Large mixing bowl

Large fork or electric mixer

Measuring cups and spoons

Plastic wrap

Spoon

Ingredients

¾ cup shortening or vegan butter

¾ cup demerara or dark brown sugar

¼ cup sugar

Pinch of salt

2 large eggs

1 tbsp honey or maple syrup

1 tsp vanilla

1 ¾ cups flour

1 tsp baking soda

1 ½ tsp baking powder

¾ cup Enjoy Life chocolate chips

Method

1. In a large bowl cream the vegan butter, sugars, salt, and honey until smooth. You can use a large fork to do this, or an electric mixer on high speed.
2. Add the vanilla and eggs and beat until well combined.
3. Add the flour, baking soda, and baking powder and mix until the dough comes together in a ball and there are no lumps of flour remaining.
4. Fold in the chocolate chips with a spoon or with your mixer on low.
5. Cover the bowl in plastic wrap and refrigerate for 2 hours.
6. When the dough is finished resting you can heat the oven to 375F. Use a regular soup spoon to scoop out lumps of dough about the size of a half-dollar and roll them into a ball with your hands. Place the balls on a baking sheet and squish them down lightly with the heel of your hand or the bottom of a glass. Space the cookies 1 inch apart to allow them to rise while baking.
7. Bake on center rack for 6 – 8 minutes depending on how soft or crunchy you prefer your cookies to be. Allow to cool on a cooling rack for 15 minutes before eating.

Makes 25 – 30 cookies

Cutout Sugar Cookie Sandwiches

Delicate sugar cookies with cut-out designs are layered with jam and sprinkled with powdered sugar to finish the look. Perfect for any tea party.

Allergen Information
This recipe does not call for any dairy, nuts, citrus, or peanuts.

Tools You Will Need
Measuring cups and spoons
Large mixing bowl
Rolling pin
Parchment paper
Fork or electric mixer
Cookie cutters – same shape in 2 sizes
Butter knife
Sifter

Ingredients
¾ cup shortening
1 ¾ cups flour
1 egg
1 tsp vanilla
A few drops any color of food coloring (optional)
A pinch of salt
½ tsp baking powder
½ cup sugar
Jam for cutouts
Powdered sugar for dusting

Method
1. In a large bowl combine the shortening, food coloring (optional), and sugar, using either a fork or electric mixer on medium-high speed, until smooth.
2. Add the vanilla and egg and beat well. The food coloring should be evenly blended in at this point.
3. Add the flour, salt, and baking powder and mix until well combined. If using an electric mixer, set at medium speed. The dough will come together in a rough clump.
4. Dump the dough onto a large sheet of parchment paper and form it into a ball with your hands. It may appear to be quite crumbly at first, but I promise it will all come together.

5. Fold it up in the parchment paper and let rest in the fridge for 2 hours.

6. After resting, the dough is ready to be rolled out. First preheat the oven to 375F. Then lightly dust the dough on all sides with flour, as well as the rolling pin and cookie cutters, to prevent sticking.

7. Roll the dough out to ¼ inch thickness.

8. You should be using at least 2 sizes of cookie cutters, preferably the same or a similar shape, so that the jam can peek out from the center of the cookie when you sandwich them together. Cut out an even number of cookies and place half of them on a baking sheet about a half inch apart. You may need to do this in two batches. Place in a preheated oven and bake for 5 – 7 minutes, until lightly golden brown. Transfer to a cooling rack and allow to rest for 15 minutes.

9. For the second half of the unbaked dough, use the smaller cookie cutter to remove the center (or off center) of the already cut cookies. Transfer the center-less cookies to a baking sheet about a half inch apart and bake for 5 – 7 minutes. Set the center cutouts aside with the other scraps which can be formed into a ball again and re-rolled.

10. Allow the top cookies to cool on a rack for 15 minutes.

11. After they're finished cooling, lay out all the bottom cookies and spread them each with a layer of jam. Strawberry is classic, but feel free to use your favorite jam, and make sure to check the ingredients prior to spreading. An all natural brand is usually safest.

12. Line up all the top cookies with cutouts on the parchment paper and give a light dusting of sugar by passing confectioner's sugar through a sifter and tapping gently with your hand.

13. Pop the top cookies onto the bottoms, matching each cookie with one closest to its shape and size (let's face it – they don't all come out looking the same).

Makes 20 sandwich cookies

Breakfast Bar Cookies

When you're rushing your kids to school in the morning, adding a healthy snack that they'll want to eat to their lunch bag may not be tops on your list. Instead of throwing in a boring apple, throw in a couple of these breakfast bar cookies. They're sweet and flavorful but also loaded with seeds, immune-boosting spices, and dried fruit. Keep some in the freezer so they're on hand in a pinch.

Allergen Information
This recipe does not call for any dairy, nuts, citrus, or peanuts.

Tools You Will Need
Large mixing bowl
Electric mixer
Measuring cups and spoons
Spoon
Baking sheet

Ingredients
2 tbsp sunflower seeds
2 tbsp pumpkin seeds

¼ cup rolled oats
½ tsp ground cinnamon
1 tsp ground ginger
Raisins
Dried cranberries
2 tbsp quinoa
1 cup Earth Balance or shortening
2 tbsp cocoa
1 ½ cups flour
½ tsp baking soda

1 tsp baking powder
¼ cup sugar
⅔ cup brown sugar
2 heaping tbsp honey
2 large eggs
Dash of salt

Method
1. Preheat oven to 375F.
2. In a large mixing bowl combine the Earth Balance or shortening, sugar, brown sugar, and honey using an electric mixer on medium speed.
3. Add the eggs and beat well.
4. Add the flour, cocoa powder, salt, cinnamon, ginger, baking powder, and baking soda and beat until well combined.
5. Set the mixer to low speed and add the sunflower seeds, pumpkin seeds, rolled oats, raisins, dried cranberries, and quinoa.
6. Use a spoon to scoop out dollops of dough the size of a half-dollar and roll each one into a ball in your hand. Space the balls 2 inches apart on a baking sheet and squish them down with the heel of your hand. They will not look completely uniform because of the various dried fruits and seeds that give them a unique, crunchy/chewy texture. These are definitely rustic looking cookies.
7. Place the baking sheet in a preheated oven and bake for 6 – 8 minutes, until lightly golden all over.

Makes 20 – 25 cookies

Sprinkle-Fun Cookies

These cookies are ideal for any birthday party (young or old)! If you like sprinkles and you like cookies, well, you're guaranteed to like these.

Allergen Information
This recipe does not call for any dairy, nuts, citrus, or peanuts.

Tools You Will Need	Ingredients
Large mixing bowl	1 cup Earth Balance or shortening
Fork	¾ cup sugar
Rolling pin	Pinch of salt
Measuring cups and spoons	1 egg
Parchment paper	1 tsp vanilla
Cookie cutter(s)	2 tbsp honey
Baking sheet	1 ¾ cups flour
	1 tsp baking powder
	2 tbsp sprinkles

Method
1. In a large mixing bowl mash the Earth Balance or shortening together with the sugar using a fork. Mash until it is creamy in texture.
2. Add the salt, egg, vanilla, honey, and beat well.
3. Add the flour, baking powder, and sprinkles all at once and mix well. The dough should come together in a rough clump at this point. You can stop mixing when all the dry ingredients are absorbed and the dough has come together in a loose ball.
4. Line your counter with a piece of parchment paper. Dump the dough out onto the parchment paper and use your hands to press it together into a square disk. Wrap the parchment around the dough and leave it to chill in the fridge for at least 2 hours.
5. When it's finished chilling, unwrap the parchment paper and dust the dough in confectioner's sugar to prevent it from sticking to the rolling pin. You can dust the rolling pin with confectioner's sugar as well. Preheat the oven to 375F.
6. Roll the dough out to ½ inch thickness and use cookie cutters to cut out shapes of your choice. You can cut out as many different shapes as you like as long as they are roughly the same size. Space the cookies 1 inch apart on a baking sheet.
7. Place the baking sheet in preheated oven and bake for 6 – 8 minutes, until lightly golden on top.

Makes 20 – 25 cookies

Apple Crisp Cookies

The beauty of an apple crisp cookie is that the less round and even it is, the better it looks.

Allergen Information
This recipe does not call for any dairy, nuts, citrus, or peanuts.

Tools You Will Need
Large mixing bowl
Electric mixer
Paring knife
Cutting board
Measuring cups and spoons
Baking sheet
Spoon

Ingredients
1 cup shortening or Earth Balance
¾ cup demerara or dark brown sugar

½ cup sugar
Pinch of salt
2 large eggs
1 tbsp honey or maple syrup
1 tsp vanilla
1 ½ cups flour
1 tsp baking soda
1 ½ tsp baking powder
1 tsp ground cinnamon
1 tsp ground ginger
¼ cup rolled oats
½ cup finely diced, peeled McIntosh apple

Method
1. Preheat oven to 375F.
2. Use a paring knife to peel, core, and finely dice the apple(s), then set aside.
3. In a large bowl cream the Earth Balance or shortening, sugars, salt, and honey or maple syrup until smooth. You can use a large fork or an electric mixer on high speed.
4. Add the vanilla and eggs and beat until well combined.
5. Add the flour, oats, baking soda, baking powder, cinnamon, and ginger, and mix until the dough comes together in a ball and there are no lumps of flour remaining.
6. Fold in the apple with a spoon or with your mixer on low.
7. Use a regular soup spoon to scoop out lumps of dough about the size of a half-dollar. Simply drop them onto a baking sheet 2 inches apart. No need to roll them out perfectly, as these are soft, chunky cookies.
8. Bake on center rack for 6 – 8 minutes depending on how soft or crunchy you prefer your cookies to be. Transfer to a cooling rack as soon as they finish baking.

Makes 25 – 30 cookies

Gingerbread Cookies

Allergen Information
This recipe does not call for any dairy, nuts, citrus, or peanuts.

Tools You Will Need

Large mixing bowl

Baking sheet

Parchment paper

Electric mixer

Cookie cutters

Measuring cups and spoons

Ingredients

⅓ cup Earth Balance or shortening

¾ cup demerara or dark brown sugar

1 tsp pure vanilla extract

1 egg

½ cup molasses

2 ¾ cups flour, plus some for dusting

2 tsp ground cinnamon

2 tsp ground ginger

½ tsp finely ground cloves

A pinch of ground cardamom (optional)

1 ½ tsp baking powder

½ tsp baking soda

A pinch of salt

Method

1. In a large mixing bowl combine the Earth Balance or shortening and sugar using an electric mixer on medium speed until fluffy.

2. Add the egg, vanilla, and molasses and beat until smooth.

3. Add the flour, cinnamon, ginger, cloves, cardamom, baking powder, baking soda, and salt and mix until well combined. Do not over mix the dough. It will come together in a clump when it's ready.

4. Dump the dough onto a large sheet of parchment paper and form it into a disk. Wrap it in parchment paper and refrigerate for 2 – 3 hours to allow it to set.

5. Once it's finished resting you can remove it from the fridge and preheat the oven to 375F. Line a baking sheet with parchment paper.

6. Dust the dough with flour or powdered sugar and roll it out to ½ inch thickness. If you prefer a crisper, crunchier cookie you can roll it out to ¼ inch thickness. Use cookie cutters to cut gingerbread people (or whatever shape you prefer) out of the dough and space them 1 inch apart on the lined baking sheet.

7. Bake for 7 – 9 minutes, until the cookies have risen and are slightly browned on top. You can allow them to cool on the parchment paper before serving.

8. Decorate with icing (see Basic Frosting recipe found on page 267) and festive sprinkles.

Makes 25 – 30 cookies

EVERYTHING CHOCOLATE

If there's one thing I've never heard a kid complain about, it's too much chocolate. I love working with chocolate because its rich and silky texture can instantly improve any dessert (and even some savory dishes). In this chapter you'll find recipes for a wide range of chocolate desserts. From decadent mousses to rich fudges and brownies; even some chocolate that you can sip on.

Hot Cocoa

A classic drink to sip on a cold day to warm you from the inside out. This version is as simple as it gets – just 3 ingredients including water.

Allergen Information
This recipe does not call for any dairy, nuts, peanuts, egg, citrus, or gluten.

Tools You Will Need
1 large mug
Kettle
Spoon

Ingredients
1 tbsp honey (use the organic stuff, it truly tastes better!)
1 ½ tbsp cocoa powder
1 ⅓ cups boiling water (about one mugful)

Method
1. Begin by putting the kettle on to boil. I like to use a stovetop kettle which takes about 7 – 10 minutes to come to a boil.
2. Use a spoon to mix the honey and cocoa powder together until it forms a loose paste. A measuring spoon isn't really necessary for this recipe; you can eyeball the measurements using your spoon and mug.
3. Pour a bit of boiling water (about ⅓ cup) into the paste and mix it vigorously until it's completely smooth. Then add the rest of the water (about 1 cup) and stir well.
4. Garnish with your preferred brand of marshmallows or a dash of ground cinnamon.

Serves 1

Hot Sipping Chocolate

A richer version of hot chocolate, this recipe only calls for 3 ingredients including melted dark chocolate. The perfect accompaniment to a family movie on a chilly day.

Allergen Information
This recipe does not call for any dairy, nuts, peanuts, egg, citrus, or gluten. Vegan.
The optional ingredient, malt, does contain gluten.

Tools You Will Need
A small saucepan
Whisk
Measuring cup
A cozy mug

Ingredients
¼ cup Enjoy Life chocolate Mega Chunks
1 cup Rice Dream (preferably vanilla)
Optional: 1 tsp malt powder

Method
1. Add the chocolate chunks and a few tbsp of the rice milk to a saucepan and turn to medium-low heat.
2. When the edges of the chocolate start to melt, begin whisking. Bubbles will form and that's perfectly okay!
3. When the chocolate has fully dissolved into the liquid, add the rest of the rice milk all at once and whisk continuously until steam starts to rise from the pan and it reaches a low boil. Be careful not to over boil or to stop whisking, as it will risk burning on the bottom.
4. Once all the rice milk is in the pan you can add a tsp of malt powder, which is a toasted oat product commonly used in English cooking. This is completely optional, but helps to round out the flavor.
5. Pour the hot sipping chocolate directly into your favorite mug and enjoy!

Serves 1

Chai Hot Chocolate

For those who crave something a little bolder, this hot chocolate mixes it up with a bit of spice.

Allergen Information
This recipe does not call for any dairy, nuts, peanuts, egg, citrus, or gluten.

Tools You Will Need
1 large mug
Kettle
Spoon

Ingredients
1 tbsp honey (use the organic stuff, it truly tastes better!)
1 ½ tbsp cocoa powder
A pinch of ground cinnamon
A pinch of ground cardamom
A pinch of ground ginger
A pinch of finely ground black pepper
½ tsp pure vanilla extract
¼ cup Rice Dream
1 cup boiling water (about one mugful)

Method
1. Put the kettle on to boil with at least 1 cup of water.
2. While the kettle is heating, combine the spices, cocoa, vanilla, and honey in a large mug. Mix it thoroughly until it forms a pasty consistency.
3. Slowly pour the rice milk in while stirring until it is well combined.
4. When the kettle has come to a boil add about 1 cup of water to the mug. This should fill it to the top.
5. Garnish with a fragrant cinnamon stick.

Serves 1

Sunbutter Chocolate Bars

With their tender, crispy inside and crunchy, chocolatey shell, these chocolate bars are sure to be a hit in any lunch box!

Allergen Information
This recipe does not call for any dairy, nuts, peanuts, citrus, or egg.
This recipe can also be made gluten-free by using gluten-free Rice Krispies.

Tools You Will Need
Small saucepan
Medium size metal mixing bowl
Wooden spoon
Square baking pan, preferably non-stick
Medium mixing bowl
Measuring cups and spoons
Chopping knife
Parchment paper
Medium-size plastic freezer bag

Ingredients
¾ cup Rice Krispies (preferably gluten-free)
1 tbsp sugar
¼ cup coconut shredded coconut (Let's Do Organic brand)
¾ cup Sunbutter
2 cups Enjoy Life chocolate chunks

Method
1. In a medium mixing bowl fold together the coconut, Sunbutter, sugar, and Rice Krispies. Feel free to use sweetened or crunchy Sunbutter. Make sure the ingredients are well combined, then set aside.
2. Pour some water in the bottom of the saucepan, about ¾ of an inch high. Then place the bowl on top of the pan and turn the heat to medium-low to create a double boiler to melt the chocolate chunks. Be sure that your bowl is completely dry before adding any chocolate.
3. Pour the chocolate chunks in and begin to lightly stir using a wooden spoon until all the chunks are melted. Once they have melted, remove the bowl from the pan immediately, as chocolate is very delicate and burns easily.
4. Line the bottom and sides of a square baking dish with parchment paper.

5. Pour about half of the chocolate into the bottom of the pan and spread it around using your wooden spoon. It doesn't have to be even or look pretty at this point, but it does have to cover the entire bottom surface of the pan in a pretty thick and even layer.

6. Next dollop scoops of the Rice Krispie mixture onto the chocolate and lightly press it out with damp fingers. If you press too hard or try to spread too much at once, you'll disrupt the layer of chocolate on the bottom.

7. Open a freezer strength plastic baggie and set it on the counter with the top folded over so it remains open. Pour the rest of the melted chocolate into the bag and seal it, squeezing out all the air as you zip it closed. Snip off the very tip with a pair of scissors. Remember, it's easier to snip a larger tip off if you find the chocolate is coming out too slowly than to deal with chocolate that is coming out too fast with a wider tip.

8. Start by zig-zagging a layer of chocolate across the top of the Rice Krispie mixture using the plastic bag like a pastry bag. Then do a zig-zag pattern in the opposite direction. Continue doing this until you have used up all the chocolate.

9. Refrigerate for at least 3 hours to let the chocolate fully harden.

10. Once chilled, remove from the fridge and pull the whole thing out of the pan by lifting out the parchment paper. Do not remove it from the parchment paper.

11. Use a chopping knife to cut the chilled dessert into squares. You can really cut them as large or as small as you like. I suggest making one cut down the middle (vertical cut) and 3 cuts across (horizontally) to make 8 bars.

12. Either serve immediately or store in the fridge until ready to serve.

Makes 8 servings

Guests : Please show t...
when making a purchas...

Bridal &
Gift Registry

Chocolate Mousse

Allergen-free chocolate mousse is nearly impossible to find at bakeries or grocery stores, so if your kids want to indulge in it you likely have to make it at home. This recipe for light-as-air mousse is sure to please. Frothy egg whites replace whipped cream to give the mousse its signature texture.

Allergen Information
This recipe does not call for any dairy, nuts, peanuts, citrus, or gluten.

Tools You Will Need
Small saucepan
Large mixing bowl
Medium metal mixing bowl
Spatula
2 cocktail glasses
Measuring cups and spoons
Electric mixer

Ingredients
3 egg whites
1 cup Enjoy Life chocolate mega chunks
1 tsp Earth Balance or shortening
2 tsp Rice Dream or Coconut Dream
1 tsp pure vanilla extract
Pinch of salt

Method
1. In a large mixing bowl use an electric mixer to beat the egg whites until they form stiff peaks. Set aside.
2. Fill a saucepan with water to a depth of 1 inch. Turn the stove to medium-low heat and place the metal mixing bowl on top. Pour the chocolate chips, vanilla, Rice or Coconut Dream, and Earth Balance or shortening in the bowl and begin to slowly stir them using a spatula once the edges of the chips start to melt. Continue to stir until the chocolate is completely melted and then immediately remove the bowl from on top of the saucepan and turn off the heat to prevent burning.
3. Scoop out about ¼ cup of chocolate and gently fold it into the egg whites, making sure to be gentle so that they don't deflate. Continue to fold the chocolate into the egg whites about ¼ cup at a time until it is fully combined.
4. Pour the mousse into cute cocktail glasses and refrigerate until firm, about 2 hours.
5. You can decorate them with mini marshmallows, sprinkles, diced fresh fruit, or chocolate shavings.

Serves 2

Chocolate Krispies on a Stick

Gluten-free rice krispies and marshmallows are great items to have on hand in the kitchen in the event that you need to accommodate a gluten intolerance at a birthday party or in school. Rice Krispie squares are a classic hit with kids and can now be easily made gluten-free. Drizzling them with chocolate and putting them on a stick makes them a bit more fun and easy to hold for little kids. You can also personalize them by adding faces and designs out of the chocolate.

Allergen Information
This recipe does not call for any dairy, nuts, citrus, or peanuts.
This recipe can be made gluten-free by using gluten-free marshmallows and Rice Krispies.
Some brands of marshmallow contain egg. Be sure to read the label if you need to accommodate an egg allergy.

Tools You Will Need
Medium pot
Baking sheet
2 sheets of parchment paper
Spatula
Candy sticks (about 20 – 30)
Cookie cutters
Small saucepan
Medium metal mixing bowl
Spoon
Freezer strength zipper bag

Ingredients
1 tbsp vegetable oil
225 – 250g marshmallows
250g Rice Krispies (preferably gluten-free)
1 cup Enjoy Life chocolate mega chunks

Method
1. Line a baking sheet with parchment paper.
2. Warm the vegetable oil in a large pot on medium heat.
3. Add the marshmallows and start stirring constantly with a wooden spoon, scraping the bottom often to make sure they don't burn. Small marshmallows work better for this because they melt much faster.

4. Once the marshmallows are melted, turn off the heat and move them to a cool burner. Then get an extra pair of hands to pour the Rice Krispies into the pot while you keep on stirring. Try to mix the ingredients in evenly by breaking up large pockets of marshmallow or cereal. The cereal should be completely coated in marshmallow.

5. As soon as the mixture is well combined, wet your fingertips with water. Dump all the Rice Krispies mixture onto the parchment lined baking sheet and use your fingers to spread it out evenly.

6. Use a cookie cutter to cut out whatever shapes you prefer. It's best to use simple shapes as more ornate ones might not translate so well in the crumply texture of the Rice Krispies. Place all the cutout shapes on a separate sheet of parchment paper.

7. Slide a candy stick into the bottom of each cut-out while they're still soft, pressing in enough that the stick can hold it up when you lift it off the parchment paper.

8. While these are cooling (and you're snacking on the leftover bits of Rice Krispie square) you can create the chocolate drizzle. Fill a saucepan with water to a depth of 1 inch. Turn the stove to medium-low heat and place the metal mixing bowl on top. Pour the chocolate chips in the bowl and begin to slowly stir them using a spatula once the edges of the chips start to melt. Continue to stir until the chocolate is completely melted and then immediately remove the bowl from on top of the saucepan and turn off the heat to prevent burning.

9. You can use a spoon to scoop the chocolate into a freezer strength zipper bag to use like a pastry bag. It'll help you get the perfect drizzle! It's important to use a freezer strength bag because the thinner sandwich bags can easily melt under the heat of the chocolate. Snip one of the corners off the bag and use it to drizzle chocolate all over the shapes. The design is up to you. You can get creative with faces, letters, dots, stripes, or whatever you can think of.

10. Allow to cool for a half hour before serving so that the chocolate can set, then allow to sit at room temperature until the Rice Krispie treat has softened up enough to bite into.

Makes 20 – 30, depending on the size of your cookie cutters

Chocolate Zabaglione

Zabaglione is a rich and silky Italian mousse that calls for marsala wine to give it a more robust flavor and to combat the thick texture created by the egg yolks. This was one of my favorite recipes to make as a kid because my family and friends always thought it was so difficult to make when in reality it is actually quite simple. The alcohol from the wine does evaporate when cooked, however, you can always substitute it for the non-alcoholic versions found in grocery stores or Coconut/Rice Dream or fruit juice.

Allergen Information
This recipe does not call for any dairy, nuts, peanuts, citrus, or gluten.

Tools You Will Need
Medium metal mixing bowl
Small saucepan
5 cocktail glasses
Paring knife
Cutting board
Measuring cups and spoons
Whisk
Handheld electric beater

Ingredients
5 egg yolks
$^1/_3$ cup marsala wine (can be substituted with Coconut
    Dream if you prefer not to use alcohol)
1 tsp vanilla
1 cup Enjoy Life chocolate chunks
1 tbsp Earth Balance
1 mango or banana

Method
1. Cut a banana, mango, or any fruit that freezes well and complements the taste of chocolate into cubes. Distribute the cubed fruit evenly into 5 cocktail glasses.
2. Fill a small saucepan with water to a depth of one inch. Then place a medium metal mixing bowl on top and turn the heat to medium-low to create a double boiler. To the mixing bowl add the egg yolks, vanilla, and marsala wine and begin to whisk immediately. The mixture will turn a pale yellow color and begin to froth and thicken. Do not stop whisking or the egg will cook and you'll end up with scrambled eggs.
3. When the mixture has about doubled in size add the chocolate, and Earth Balance and continue to whisk. Both will gradually melt into the egg mixture. As soon as all the chocolate has melted and the batter is creamy and even in color, take the bowl off the saucepan and turn off the heat.
4. Pour or scoop the chocolate zabaglione into each cocktail glass on top of the fruit and refrigerate for 3 hours to allow it to fully set. If you want to serve this dessert at room temperature, take it out of the freezer 20 – 25 minutes before you are ready to serve.

Serves 5

Fudgy Brownies

You'll notice that there are several brownie recipes in this book, all of which are totally different. This particular recipe produces rich, dense brownies with a ton of melted chocolate and very little flour by comparison. Try out all the brownie recipes to see which one is your favorite!

Allergen Information
This recipe does not call for any dairy, nuts, citrus, or peanuts.

Tools You Will Need
Small saucepan
Large metal mixing bowl
Spatula
Whisk
Glass baking dish
Parchment paper
Measuring cups and spoons

Ingredients
1 cup Enjoy Life chocolate chips
5 tbsp Earth Balance or shortening
2 large eggs
$^2/_3$ cup sugar
1 tsp vanilla
¾ cup flour
2 tbsp cocoa powder

Method
1. Preheat oven to 350F and line a square glass baking dish with parchment paper.
2. Fill a small saucepan to a depth of one inch with water and place the mixing bowl on top to create a double boiler. Turn the heat to medium-low.
3. Add the chocolate chips, vanilla, and Earth Balance or shortening to the bowl and begin to stir with a spatula until all the chocolate is melted. Remove the bowl from the saucepan immediately and turn the heat off.
4. Add the eggs to the chocolate mixture one at a time and begin to beat well with a whisk until the eggs are well combined.
5. Add the sugar and beat well.
6. Add the cocoa powder and flour and fold together with a spatula, making sure all the dry ingredients are fully dissolved. You can fold in some extra chocolate chips at this point if you desire.
7. Pour the batter into the lined glass baking dish and smooth out the top with a spatula. Place the baking dish in preheated oven and bake for 25 – 35 minutes, until a toothpick inserted in center comes out clean.

Serves 8

Egg-Free Brownies

This is a recipe for what I call "cakey brownies," meaning that they have a sort of cake-like texture and are less dense than the chocolate-packed fudgy brownies.

Allergen Information
This recipe does not call for any dairy, nuts, peanuts, citrus, or egg.

Tools You Will Need
Whisk
Large mixing bowl
8 inch round or square pan
Parchment paper
Measuring cups and spoons

Ingredients
½ cup applesauce
⅓ cup vegetable oil
1 tsp pure vanilla extract
Pinch of salt
½ cup Coconut Dream
¾ cup sugar
⅓ cup cocoa powder
1 tsp baking powder
½ tsp baking soda
1 ½ cups all purpose flour
⅓ cup Enjoy Life mini chocolate chips

Method
1. Preheat oven to 375F and line baking pan with parchment paper.
2. In a large mixing bowl combine the applesauce, oil, vanilla, salt, coconut milk, and sugar using a whisk. Beat until well combined.
3. Add the cocoa powder, flour, baking soda, baking powder, and chocolate chips and beat until smooth.
4. Pour the batter into baking dish and smooth out the top.
5. Place the pan in preheated oven and bake for 30 – 35 minutes, until toothpick insterted in center comes out clean.

Serves 8

Gluten-Free Brownies

Allergen Information
This recipe does not call for any dairy, nuts, peanuts, citrus, or gluten.

Tools You Will Need
Small saucepan
Large metal mixing bowl
Spatula
Whisk
Glass baking dish
Parchment paper
Measuring cups and spoons

Ingredients
1 cup Enjoy Life chocolate chips
2 tbsp Earth Balance or shortening
2 large eggs
2 tbsp Rice Dream or Coconut Dream
¾ cup sugar
1 tsp vanilla
½ cup plus 1 tbsp Let's Do Organic coconut flour
1 tbsp cocoa powder
Pinch of salt

Method
1. Preheat oven to 350F and line a square glass baking dish with parchment paper.
2. Fill a small saucepan to a depth of one inch with water and place the mixing bowl on top to create a double boiler. Turn the heat to medium-low.
3. Add the chocolate chips, vanilla, and Earth Balance or shortening to the bowl and begin to stir with a spatula until all the chocolate is melted. Remove the bowl from the saucepan immediately and turn the heat off.
4. Add the eggs to the chocolate mixture one at a time and begin to beat well with a whisk until the eggs are well combined.
5. Add the sugar and beat well.
6. Add the cocoa powder, salt, and coconut flour and fold together with a spatula, making sure all the dry ingredients are fully dissolved. You can fold in some extra chocolate chips at this point if you desire.
7. Pour the batter into the lined glass baking dish and smooth out the top with a spatula. Place the baking dish in preheated oven and bake for 25 – 35 minutes, until a toothpick inserted in center comes out clean.

Serves 8

Chocolate Covered Fruit Skewers

Allergen Information
This recipe does not call for any dairy, nuts, peanuts, egg, citrus, or gluten.

Tools You Will Need
6 – 8 bamboo skewers

Measuring cup

Medium metal mixing bowl

Small saucepan

Spatula

Freezer strength plastic zipper bag

Paring knife

Cutting board

Parchment paper

Baking sheet

Ingredients
1 lb strawberries

2 bananas

1 ½ cups Enjoy Life chocolate chunks

Sprinkles or shredded coconut flakes (optional)

Method
1. Use a paring knife to slice the bananas into ½ inch thick rounds, and to chop the leafy greens off the strawberries. Set aside. Place the skewers in the fridge.
2. The chocolate chips can be melted using a double boiler. Fill a saucepan with water to a depth of 1 inch. Turn the stove to medium-low heat and place the metal mixing bowl on top. Pour the chocolate chips in the bowl and begin to slowly stir them using a spatula once the edges of the chips start to melt. Continue to stir until the chocolate is completely melted and then immediately remove the bowl from on top of the saucepan and turn off the heat to prevent burning.
3. When the chocolate has set after an hour, remove the skewers from the fridge. Slide 1 each of the fruits onto each skewer in whatever order you like. There's no right or wrong way to do this! Each skewer can look different, or they can all look the same. You can also replace any of the fruits with ones that are local to your area, in season, or just happen to be your favorites.
4. You can add a dusting of shredded coconut flakes or sprinkles at this point so they will stick to the chocolate covered areas. Refrigerate the skewers until ready to serve.

Serves 6 – 8

Maple Chocolate Fudge

Allergen Information

This recipe does not call for any dairy, nuts, peanuts, egg, citrus, or gluten.

Tools You Will Need

Small loaf pan

Parchment paper

Medium metal mixing bowl

Small saucepan

Whisk

Measuring cups and spoons

Mixing spoon

Ingredients

1 cup Enjoy Life chocolate chunks

¼ cup maple syrup

½ tsp pure vanilla extract

3 tbsp Earth Balance or shortening

Cinnamon for sprinkling

Method

1. Line the loaf pan with parchment paper along the bottom and sides.
2. Fill a saucepan with water to a depth of 1 inch. Turn the stove to medium-low heat and place the metal mixing bowl on top. Pour the chocolate chips, vanilla, maple syrup, and Earth Balance in the bowl and begin to slowly stir using a spatula once the edges of the chips start to melt. Once the chips begin to melt, begin to beat using a whisk until the chocolate is completely melted and then immediately remove the bowl from on top of the saucepan and turn off the heat to prevent burning.
3. Pour the chocolate into the lined loaf pan and smooth out the top with a spoon.
4. Refrigerate for 3 hours to allow it to fully set before slicing.
5. Sprinkle it with a bit of cinnamon before slicing to add some visual appeal.

Makes about 10 slices of fudge

Chocolate Sunbutter Fudge

Allergen Information
This recipe does not call for any dairy, nuts, peanuts, egg, citrus, or gluten.

Tools You Will Need
Small loaf pan
Parchment paper
Medium metal mixing bowl
Small saucepan
Whisk
Measuring cups and spoons
Mixing spoon

Ingredients
1 cup Enjoy Life chocolate chunks
2 tbsp brown sugar
½ tsp pure vanilla extract
3 tbsp Earth Balance or shortening
¼ cup Sunbutter

Method
1. Line the loaf pan with parchment paper along the bottom and sides.
2. Fill a saucepan with water to a depth of 1 inch. Turn the stove to medium-low heat and place the metal mixing bowl on top. Pour the chocolate chips, vanilla, brown sugar, and Earth Balance in the bowl and begin to slowly stir using a spatula once the edges of the chips start to melt. Once the chips begin to melt, begin to beat using a whisk until the chocolate is completely melted and then immediately remove the bowl from on top of the saucepan and turn off the heat to prevent burning.
3. Spoon in the Sunbutter and swirl it around. You can fully combine it by beating with a whisk, or you can just swirl it around so that it stands out.
4. Pour the chocolate mixture into the lined loaf pan and smooth out the top with a spoon.
5. Refrigerate for 3 hours to allow it to fully set before slicing.

Makes about 10 slices of fudge

Chocolate Marshmallow Fudge

Allergen Information

This recipe does not call for any dairy, nuts, peanuts, egg, or gluten.

Be sure to use marshmallows that are marked gluten-free. Some brands of marshmallows contain egg, so be sure to read the label.

Tools You Will Need

Small loaf pan

Parchment paper

Medium metal mixing bowl

Small saucepan

Whisk

Measuring cups and spoons

Mixing spoon

Ingredients

1 cup Enjoy Life chocolate chunks

2 tbsp brown sugar

½ tsp pure vanilla extract

3 tbsp Earth Balance or shortening

¾ cup marshmallows

*Although marshmallows are generally free of dairy and nuts, be sure to read the label before using them in this recipe.

Method

1. Line the loaf pan with parchment paper along the bottom and sides.
2. Fill a saucepan with water to a depth of 1 inch. Turn the stove to medium-low heat and place the metal mixing bowl on top. Pour the chocolate chips, vanilla, brown sugar, and Earth Balance in the bowl and begin to slowly stir using a spatula once the edges of the chips start to melt. Once the chips begin to melt, begin to beat using a whisk until the chocolate is completely melted and then immediately remove the bowl from on top of the saucepan and turn off the heat to prevent burning.
3. Add the marshmallows to the chocolate mixture and mix well using a spoon. If you prefer the fudge to be more chocolatey than marshmallowy you can just add ½ cup instead of ¾ cup of marshmallows.
4. Pour the chocolate mixture into the lined loaf pan and smooth out the top with a spoon.
5. Refrigerate for 3 hours to allow it to fully set before slicing.
6. You can sprinkle some marshmallows on top of the fudge before refrigerating for decoration if you desire.

Makes about 10 slices of fudge

Coconut Fudge

Allergen Information
This recipe does not call for any dairy, nuts, peanuts, egg, citrus, or gluten.

Tools You Will Need
Small loaf pan
Parchment paper
Medium metal mixing bowl
Small saucepan
Whisk
Measuring cups and spoons
Mixing spoon

Ingredients
1 cup Enjoy Life chocolate chunks
2 tbsp brown sugar
½ tsp pure vanilla extract
3 tbsp Earth Balance or shortening
1/3 cup Let's Do Organic dried, shredded coconut

Method
1. Line the loaf pan with parchment paper along the bottom and sides.
2. Fill a saucepan with water to a depth of 1 inch. Turn the stove to medium-low heat and place the metal mixing bowl on top. Pour the chocolate chips, vanilla, brown sugar, and Earth Balance in the bowl and begin to slowly stir using a spatula once the edges of the chips start to melt. Once the chips begin to melt, begin to beat using a whisk until the chocolate is completely melted and then immediately remove the bowl from on top of the saucepan and turn off the heat to prevent burning.
3. Add the coconut to the chocolate mixture and mix well using a spoon. The amount of coconut to add is flexible, so feel free to add more or less according to your tastes.
4. Pour the chocolate mixture into the lined loaf pan and smooth out the top with a spoon.
5. Refrigerate for 3 hours to allow it to fully set before slicing.
6. You can sprinkle some coconut on top of the fudge before refrigerating for decoration if you desire.

*Try Earth Balance Coconut Spread for this recipe to maximize the coconut flavor!

Makes about 10 slices of fudge

✤ SCONES

Simple scone dough can be adapted for a medley of different desserts and snacks. Basic scones are always delicious, but why not change up the flavor by adding fresh fruits and zests? Or use it as a crust for a sweet pizza, or a flaky pastry shell? What I love most about scone dough is that it is really simple and quick to prepare and can be matched with almost any flavor palate whether it be sweet or savory. People always remark that they can't believe I just made scones from scratch, but little do they know it only takes 20 minutes from start to finish.

Scones

Scones are a staple food at any tea party or garden party. They can be coated in sugar before baking, dyed pastel pink, or cut into fun shapes. Their simplicity is what makes them so wonderfully timeless. Try serving them with Coconut Cream drizzle and fruit, or with freshly made Strawberry Jam. If you reduce the sugar to 1 tbsp you can make savory biscuits that go great with soups and stews. Scones and biscuits were always a real hit in my house growing up, and one of the recipes my mom mastered because she could not find an allergen-free alternative in stores.

Allergen Information
This recipe does not call for any dairy, nuts, peanuts, citrus, or egg.

Tools You Will Need
Large mixing bowl
Measuring cups and spoons
Mixing spoon
Parchment paper
Baking sheet
Water glass or paring knife

Ingredients
2 cups of flour
$^1/_3$ cup Earth Balance or shortening
¼ cup confectioner's sugar
Pinch of salt
3 tsp baking powder
1 tsp pure vanilla extract
$^2/_3$ cup water or Rice Dream (vanilla flavor works well)

Method
1. Preheat oven to 400F.
2. In a large mixing bowl combine the flour, sugar, baking powder, and salt.
3. Add the shortening or Earth Balance and mash it into the dry ingredients using a fork, breaking it down into little pea-sized pieces.
4. Form a well in the center of the dry mixture and add the vanilla and water or rice milk. Slowly begin folding the flour into the wet ingredients until it starts coming together in a loose dough. You can stop mixing when it starts coming together in large clumps and the wet ingredients have been absorbed.

5. Tear off a large piece of parchment paper to line your counter. Dump the dough onto the paper and use your hands to form it into a ball.

6. Begin kneading the dough by folding it in half and then pressing it down with the heal of your hand. Repeat this 8 times. You may want to use an extra dusting of flour to coat your work surface or the dough if it becomes sticky.

7. Dust the dough and your rolling pin with flour. Roll the dough out to ½ inch thickness and use either the mouth of a glass to cut it into circles (the size of circle is up to you) or a paring knife to cut it into squares.

8. Space the scones on a baking sheet about 1 ½ inches apart. You can brush them with Rice Dream and sprinkle the tops with sugar at this point if you desire.

9. Place the baking sheet on the center rack of your preheated oven and bake for 8 – 10 minutes, until golden brown on top.

Makes 12 – 15 scones

Strawberry Stuffed Scones

Light and flaky scone pastry with a center full of homemade strawberry jam. The filling can be changed according to which fruits are in season. This is simple comfort food at its best.

This recipe does not call for any dairy, nuts, peanuts, or egg.

Tools You Will Need

Large mixing bowl

Measuring cups and spoons

Rolling pin

Large fork

Parchment paper

Large round cookie cutter or a wide-mouthed water glass

12 cup muffin pan

Ingredients

2 cups flour

4 heaping tbsp confectioner's sugar

Pinch of salt

½ tsp baking soda

2 tsp baking powder

1 tsp cream of tartar

²/₃ cup shortening or Earth Balance vegan butter

¾ cup water or rice milk

¹/₃ cup strawberry jam (found on page 249)

Method

1. Preheat oven to 400F.
2. In a large mixing bowl combine the flour, sugar, baking powder, baking soda, and salt.
3. Add the shortening or vegan butter and mash it into the flour using a fork, breaking it down into little pea-sized pieces.
4. Form a well in the center of the dry mixture and add the water or rice milk. Slowly begin folding the flour into the wet ingredients until it starts coming together in a loose dough. You can stop mixing when it starts coming together in large clumps and the wet ingredients have been absorbed.
5. Tear off a large piece of parchment paper to line your counter. Dump the dough onto the paper and use your hands to form it into a ball.
6. Begin kneading the dough by folding it in half and then pressing it down with the heal of your hand. Repeat this 8 times.
7. Dust the dough and your rolling pin with flour. Roll the dough out to ½ inch thickness.
8. Use either a large (approx. 2 ½ inches in diameter) round cookie cutter or the mouth of a water glass to cut out circles of dough. Press each circle of dough into a cup in your muffin pan. Use your fingers to press it up the sides to create a deeper cup. If you roll the dough too thinly, there will not be enough excess to press it up the sides and the shell will be too short to hold the filling.
9. Scoop out about 1 tbsp of jam (recipe found on page 249) for each cup, making sure that it does not spill over the sides.
10. Place in your preheated oven and bake for 10 – 12 minutes, until the edges of the dough are golden brown.
11. Allow to cool before removing the tarts from the pan. Remove them by simply running a fork around the edge of the tart and lifting it out.

Fruit Pizza

Personal fruit pizzas are a great party craft for small groups of little kids. The dough and toppings can be prepared ahead of time and the kids can each roll out their own pizza crust and fill it with toppings. This dessert is healthier than a slice of cake but also allows the kids to add their own personal touch of creativity. It can also be made into 1 or 2 large portions and sliced like a real pizza depending on your preference and how much time you have on hand.

This recipe does not call for any dairy, nuts, peanuts, citrus, or egg.
Some brands of marshmallow do contain egg, so be sure to read the label if you need to accommodate an egg allergy.

Tools You Will Need
Large mixing bowl
Measuring cups and spoons
Mixing spoon
Parchment paper
Baking sheet
Paring knife and cutting board

Ingredients
2 cups of flour
$^1/_3$ cup Earth Balance or shortening
¼ cup confectioner's sugar
Pinch of salt
2 tsp baking powder
1 tsp pure vanilla extract
$^2/_3$ cup water or Rice Dream (vanilla flavor works well)
1 cup mini marshmallows
About 2 cups of sliced/diced mixed berries and ripe fruits
¼ cup Enjoy Life mini chocolate chips

Method

1. Preheat oven to 400F.
2. In a large mixing bowl combine the flour, sugar, baking powder, and salt.
3. Add the shortening or Earth Balance and mash it into the dry ingredients using a fork, breaking it down into little pea-sized pieces.
4. Form a well in the center of the dry mixture and add the vanilla and water or rice milk. Slowly begin folding the flour into the wet ingredients until it starts coming together in a loose dough. You can stop mixing when it starts coming together in large clumps and the wet ingredients have been absorbed.
5. Tear off a large piece of parchment paper to line your counter. Dump the dough onto the paper and use your hands to form it into a ball.
6. Begin kneading the dough by folding it in half and then pressing it down with the heal of your hand. Repeat this 8 times. You may want to use an extra dusting of flour to coat your work surface or the dough if it becomes sticky.
7. Dust the dough and your rolling pin with flour. Cut the dough into 6 portions and form each one into a ball. Roll each ball out to a ½ inch thick circle.
8. Space the mini pizza crusts on a baking sheet about 1 ½ inches apart.
9. Decorate the crusts with diced up berries, mini chocolate chips, and even some jam spread on the base to look like sauce.
10. Place the baking sheet on the center rack of your preheated oven and bake for 8 – 10 minutes, until golden brown on the edges and the fruit has softened. At this point you can add the mini marshmallows (to act as the "cheese") and pop it back in the oven for about 30 seconds. Keep a close eye on it because marshmallows turn from golden to burnt fairly quickly.

Makes approximately 6 fruit pizzas

Cinnamon Biscuit Buns

Flaky biscuits and spicy cinnamon buns collide to make this crowd-pleaser of a dessert. I came up with this recipe sort of by accident one day when I was craving cinnamon buns but didn't have any yeast on hand so I had to improvise by altering my recipe for scones.

Allergen Information
This recipe does not call for any dairy, nuts, citrus, or peanuts.

Tools You Will Need
12 cup muffin pan
Parchment paper
Large mixing bowl
Dinner fork
Paper muffin liners
Rolling pin
Non-serrated knife

Ingredients
$^2/_3$ cup vegan butter or shortening or lard
2 cups flour
¼ cup confectioner's sugar
Pinch of salt
1 tsp ground cinnamon
½ tsp baking soda
3 tsp baking powder
3 egg yolks
½ cup cold water
4 heaping tbsp brown sugar
1 tsp cinnamon for dusting
Pinch of salt for dusting

Method
1. Preheat oven to 400F and line a muffin pan with paper muffin liners.
2. Add the vegan butter (or shortening or lard), flour, confectioner's sugar, salt, baking soda, baking powder, and cinnamon to the large mixing bowl. Use a dinner fork to break up the vegan butter into small pieces, the size of peas, and mix together with the flour. Make sure all the ingredients are well combined.

3. Make a well in the center of the dry ingredients and add the yolks and water. Begin slowly mixing the dry ingredients into the wet ingredients. Continue mixing until it has formed a dough.

4. Lay out a sheet of parchment paper on the counter and dump the dough onto it. Use your (clean and dry) hands to form it into a mound. Now you are going to knead the dough 8 times. To knead the dough, first use the heel of your hand to flatten the dough into a fat disk. Then fold it in half and use the heel of your hand to flatten it down. To knead it a second time, fold the dough in the opposite direction and flatten it out with the heel of your hand. Repeat this until you have kneaded the dough 8 times. Kneading creates layers that will puff up and become flaky while the dough is in the oven.

5. Lightly dust the dough with flour and use your rolling pin to roll it out to a ½ inch thick rectangular shape. Sprinkle the brown sugar, cinnamon, and salt over the rolled out dough. Use a fork or spoon to spread it evenly over the surface. Then begin rolling the dough until it is one long cylinder.

6. Use a non-serrated knife to slice the roll into ½ inch thick slices, making sure to cut back and forth through the dough instead of pressing down onto it. A non-serrated knife is a knife with no ridges along the bottom. It will slide more smoothly through the dough.

7. Place each slice of cinnamon roll face up into a lined muffin cup. Place the tray into your preheated oven and bake for 10 minutes. When they are done you can turn them upside down so that all the melted sugar is on top, and can even sprinkle with more cinnamon!

Makes 12 cinnamon buns

Lemon Blueberry Scones

Incorporate fresh blueberries and tart lemon zest into a basic scone recipe that's perfect for an after-school snack or with breakfast.

Allergen Information
This recipe does not call for any dairy, nuts, or peanuts.

Tools You Will Need
Parchment paper
Baking sheet
Large mixing bowl
Dinner fork
Rolling pin
Non-serrated knife or round cookie cutter
Small bowl
Pastry brush or silicone brush
Zester

Ingredients
2 cups flour
3 heaping tbsp sugar
Pinch of salt
½ tsp baking soda
4 tsp baking powder
1 tsp cream of tartar
The zest of half a lemon
²/₃ cup shortening
½ tsp pure vanilla extract
¾ cup cold water
1 tbsp honey
¾ cup blueberries
1 large egg

Method
1. Preheat the oven to 400F and line a baking sheet with parchment paper (if you plan to use egg wash).
2. Wash and pat dry the blueberries and set aside.

3. Wash and pat dry the lemon. Run a fine zester along the skin of the lemon, making sure to avoid the layer of pith underneath. It's a good idea to do this over a bowl. Set the zest aside.

4. In a large bowl combine the flour, baking soda, baking powder, cream of tartar, lemon zest, sugar, and salt using a dinner fork.

5. Add the shortening to the mixture and mash it using a fork until it has formed small lumps, roughly the size of peas.

6. Make a well in the center of the mixture and add the vanilla, water, honey, and blueberries all at once. Begin to fold the ingredients together using a fork.

7. Continue folding until slightly sticky dough has formed. Roll out a large piece of parchment paper and dust with flour. Turn the dough out onto the parchment paper. Then dust the top with a bit of flour.

8. Knead the dough 8 – 10 times and then press flat with the palm of your hand.

9. Now use your rolling pin to roll the dough out to a ½ inch thickness.

10. Use a non-serrated knife to cut the dough into squares, or a round cookie cutter to make circles. If you don't have a round cookie cutter you can use a water glass turned upside down.

11. Place the scones 1 inch apart on the baking sheet.

12. To make an egg wash crack one large egg into a small bowl and beat with a fork. You can use the same fork that you mixed your dough with. Then dip a pastry or silicone brush into the egg and lightly brush it over the tops of the scones.

13. Place the baking sheet in the oven and bake for 11 – 15 minutes. The tops will be slightly golden brown when they are finished.

Makes 15 scones

Orange Cranberry Scones

The flavors of orange and cranberry make these scones a great accompaniment to any holiday feast.

Allergen Information

This recipe does not call for any dairy, nuts, peanuts, or egg.

Tools You Will Need

Parchment paper

Baking sheet

Large mixing bowl

Dinner fork

Small bowl

Ingredients

2 cups flour

4 heaping tbsp confectioner's sugar

Pinch of salt

½ tsp baking soda

4 tsp baking powder

1 tsp cream of tartar

½ cup shortening

½ tsp pure vanilla extract

¼ cup cold water

½ cup orange juice

¹/₃ cup dried cranberries

¼ tsp ground cinnamon

½ cup sugar

Method

1. Preheat oven to 400F.
2. In a large mixing bowl combine the flour, confectioner's sugar, salt, baking soda, baking powder, cream of tartar, and cinnamon using a fork.
3. Add the shortening and mash it with a fork until it has formed small lumps roughly the size of peas.
4. Make a well in the center of the mixture and add the orange juice, water, vanilla, and cranberries all at once. Fold the mixture together using a fork until it becomes a crumbly dough.
5. Roll out a large sheet of parchment paper and dust with a bit of flour. Turn the dough out onto the parchment paper and use your clean hands to form it into a ball.
6. Knead the dough 8 – 10 times and then press it flat with your palm.
7. Pour the sugar into a small bowl and set aside.
8. Tear off chunks of dough about half the size of your palm. Roll each piece into a ball and pinch the end. The tighter it is rolled, the better it will stay together while baking.
9. Roll each ball in the sugar and place on a baking sheet one inch apart.
10. Place the baking sheet in the oven and bake for 8 – 10 minutes.

Makes 15 scones

Chocolate Scone Bites

Scones infused with dark cocoa are wonderfully light and airy in texture, and rich and delicious in flavor. These little bites can prove to be seriously addictive.

Allergen Information
This recipe does not call for any dairy, nuts, peanuts, citrus, or egg.

Tools You Will Need
Large mixing bowl
Measuring cups and spoons
Mixing spoon
Parchment paper
Baking sheet
Water glass or paring knife

Ingredients
1 ¾ cups of flour
¼ cup cocoa powder
¹/₃ cup Earth Balance or shortening
¼ cup sugar
Pinch of salt
3 tsp baking powder
1 tsp pure vanilla extract
²/₃ cup water or Rice Dream (vanilla flavor works well)
¼ cup Enjoy Life mini chocolate chips

Method
1. Preheat oven to 400F.
2. In a large mixing bowl combine the flour, cocoa, sugar, baking powder, and salt.
3. Add the shortening or Earth Balance and mash it into the dry ingredients using a fork, breaking it down into little pea-sized pieces.
4. Form a well in the center of the dry mixture and add the vanilla, chocolate chips, and water or rice milk. Slowly begin folding the flour into the wet ingredients until it starts coming together in a loose dough. You can stop mixing when it starts coming together in large clumps and the wet ingredients have been absorbed.
5. Tear off a large piece of parchment paper to line your counter. Dump the dough onto the paper and use your hands to form it into a ball.

6. Begin kneading the dough by folding it in half and then pressing it down with the heel of your hand. Repeat this 6 times. You may want to use an extra dusting of flour to coat your work surface or the dough if it becomes sticky.

7. Dust the dough and your rolling pin with flour. Roll the dough out to ½ inch thickness and use either the mouth of a glass to cut it into circles (the size of circle is up to you) or a paring knife to cut it into squares.

8. Space the scones on a baking sheet about 1 ½ inches apart. You can brush them with Rice Dream and sprinkle the tops with sugar at this point if you desire.

9. Place the baking sheet on the center rack of your preheated oven and bake for 8 – 10 minutes, until golden brown on top.

Makes 15 – 18 scones

Toaster Strudels

With flaky pastry and a gooey center, these strudels could fit for breakfast *or* dessert (or maybe both).

Allergen Information
This recipe does not call for any dairy, nuts, or peanuts.

Tools You Will Need
Large mixing bowl
Measuring cups and spoons
Mixing spoon
Parchment paper
Baking sheet
Paring knife
Pastry brush
Small bowl
Rolling pin

Ingredients
Dough part 1:
2 cups of flour

1 cup Earth Balance or shortening
¼ cup sugar
¼ tsp salt
2 tsp baking powder
½ cup water
2 egg yolks

Dough part 2:
¾ cup Earth Balance or shortening
¾ cup flour
Pinch of salt
1 cup jam (found on page 249)
1 egg for egg wash

Method
1. Preheat oven to 400F.
2. In a large mixing bowl combine the flour, sugar, baking powder, and salt.
3. Add the shortening or Earth Balance and mash it into the dry ingredients using a fork, breaking it down into little pea-sized pieces.
4. Form a well in the center of the dry mixture and add the vanilla and water or rice milk. Slowly begin folding the flour into the wet ingredients until it starts coming together in a loose dough. You can stop mixing when it starts coming together in large clumps and the wet ingredients have been absorbed.
5. Tear off a large piece of parchment paper to line your counter. Dump the dough onto the paper and use your hands to form it into a ball.
6. Begin kneading the dough by folding it in half and then pressing it down with the heel of your hand. Repeat this 8 times. You may want to use an extra dusting of flour to coat your work surface or the dough if it becomes sticky. Form it into a disk and wrap the parchment paper around it, then place in the fridge.
7. In a large mixing bowl again add the ingredients listed for part 2 of the dough: Earth Balance or shortening, flour, and salt. Use a fork to mash everything well until it comes together in a ball.

8. Tear off a sheet of parchment paper and dump the dough out onto it. Form it into a disk and wrap the parchment paper around it, then place it in the fridge.

9. Leave both portions of dough in the fridge for an hour to rest.

10. After resting pull out the first batch of dough. Roll it out into a square about a ¼ inch thick. Use your hands to slightly flatten out the second ball of dough and place it in the center of the rolled out dough. Fold the edges of the first dough over it like a pouch. Then dust your rolling pin with flour and roll it all out to a ½ inch thickness.

11. Fold the dough in half and roll it to a ½ inch thickness again. Repeat this 3 more times. This creates flaky layers in the pastry.

12. Dust the dough and your rolling pin with flour. Roll the dough out to ¼ inch thickness and shape it as much like a rectangle as possible, keeping it about 8 inches wide.

13. Drop 1 tbsp dollops of cold jam along half the length of dough, spacing them about 2 inches apart and leaving an inch border around the edge. Do this to only one half of the length of dough, then fold the other half over the jam-dolloped half. You will have a series of dough-covered jam pockets. Use your hands to press in between the jam dollops to seal the two sheets of dough together.

14. Use either the mouth of a glass to cut it into circles (the size of circle is up to you) or a paring knife to cut the sheet of dough into squares, leaving even space between each dollop of jam. Use a fork to crimp the edges and keep the dough sealed shut while baking.

15. Space the scones on a baking sheet about 1 ½ inches apart. You can brush them with Rice Dream and sprinkle the tops with sugar at this point if you desire, or you can brush them with egg wash.

16. Place the baking sheet on the center rack of your preheated oven and bake for 18 – 20 minutes, until golden brown on top.

Makes 12 – 15 scones

PIES AND CRUMBLES

Finding allergen-free pies and crumbles in grocery stores these days is like searching for a needle in a haystack. And truth be told, the best pies are the ones made at home. You can customize the amount of crust and filling you use, as well as the flavors, sweetness, and chunkiness of the filling. In my opinion, the best part is customizing the top crust. I always slice 3 slits in my top crust and I like to add pastry leaves and hearts for extra decoration if it's a special occasion. What will your signature crust look like?

Raspberry Meringue Tart

The sweetness of the meringue and the richness of the crust are offset by the tartness of the raspberries that are sandwiched between. This dish presents beautifully and is a lighter and less sweet alternative to pie. It is also much faster to prepare and takes less time to cool. This tart is a great option for beginner bakers because the shortbread crust is super easy to assemble and the filling is added raw so there are fewer steps for preparation and assembly. I would suggest serving this tart at a summer picnic or barbeque as it transports very easily, can be made ahead, and is best served cold.

Allergen Information
This recipe does not call for any dairy, nuts, citrus, or peanuts.

Tools You Will Need
Large metal mixing bowl
Medium mixing bowl
Electric mixer
Fork
Pie pan
Spoon
Measuring cups and spoons

Ingredients
½ cup Earth Balance or shortening
1 egg yolk
½ cup sugar
1 cup all purpose flour
Pinch of salt

Sugar for dusting berries
1 ½ pints of raspberries

4 egg whites
½ tsp cream of tartar
1 heaping tbsp confectioner's sugar

Method

1. Preheat oven to 400F.

2. In a medium mixing bowl mash the egg, sugar, salt, and Earth Balance or shortening using a fork. Mix until creamy.

3. Fold in the flour until the mixture has formed into a bunch of little pea-sized balls of dough. It's a very crumbly dough so don't be alarmed that it's not coming together in a ball.

4. Transfer all the dough at once into the pie pan and use either your fingers or the bottom of a measuring cup to press it well into the sides and bottom of the pan. It's okay to leave the edges around the brim of the pan a little rough; it adds some rustic charm.

5. Place the pie pan in the preheated oven and bake for 10 – 12 minutes, until lightly golden.

6. After removing the tart crust from the oven, turn the temperature down to 350F.

7. After washing your raspberries, make sure they are completely dry or else they will cause the crust to become soggy. Fill the tart crust by lining the berries along the edge, with bottoms facing up, in a tight circle until you reach the middle. Set aside.

8. In a large metal mixing bowl beat the egg whites and cream of tartar on high speed using an electric mixer until they form stiff peaks. You can test if they have formed stiff peaks by dipping one of the beater whisks into the egg white and turning it so that the peak is in the air. If the peak stands upright, it is ready and you can stop beating.

9. Once the right consistency is reached you can add the confectioner's sugar and beat until it's well combined. If the confectioner's sugar is lumpy it's a good idea to pass it through a sifter before adding to the whites. Use a soup spoon to transfer fluffy dollops of meringue on top of the raspberries, trying not to leave too many gaps in between scoops.

10. Place the tart on the middle rack of the 350F oven and bake for 8 – 10 minutes, until the peaks of the meringue clouds have browned to a nice golden color.

11. Allow the tart to chill for an hour. Dust berries before serving.

Serves 8 – 10

Chocolate Mousse and Cookie Tart

Next time you whip up a batch of fudgy sandwich cookies, keep about half of the unfilled cookies in a plastic zipper bag in your freezer so that you can quickly whip up this chocolatey tart on demand. This recipe is for true chocolate lovers and combines a decadent cookie crust with a rich chocolate mousse filling. It is best served chilled or at room temperature with raspberries or strawberries. This tart is the epitome of richness.

Allergen Information
This recipe does not call for any dairy, nuts, citrus, or peanuts.

Tools You Will Need
2 medium metal mixing bowls
Small saucepan
Whisk
Measuring cups and spoons
Large plastic zipper bag
Fork
Parchment paper
Square glass baking dish

Ingredients
2 cups chocolate cookie crumbs (see Fudgy Sandwich Cookie recipe on page 71)
1/3 cup Earth Balance or shortening

2 egg yolks
1 cup Enjoy Life chocolate chips
1 tsp pure vanilla extract
1/3 cup Coconut Dream
1 tsp Earth Balance

*If there is an egg allergy, you can easily substitute the egg yolks with 1 tbsp Earth Balance or shortening and 2 tbsp extra Coconut Dream.

* In a pinch you can use graham crackers in place of chocolate cookies for the crust

Method

1. Preheat oven to 400F and line a square glass baking dish with parchment paper on both the sides and bottom.

2. Using the cookie portion of the Fudgy Sandwich Cookie recipe found in this book you will make the bottom crust. Place the cookies in a large plastic zipper bag and seal it shut. Then use your hands to smash the cookies into tiny crumbs. Pour the crumbs into a medium mixing bowl and add the Earth Balance or shortening. If you have just above or under 2 cups of crumbs that's perfectly fine. Use a fork to mash the Earth Balance into the crumbs, and then get in there with your hands to really combine the two together. The mixture will feel kind of like oily soil at this point.

3. Turn the crumb mixture onto the lined baking dish and use your fingers to press it down flat, making sure to get it right to the edges. You can use a measuring cup to get it perfectly smooth.

4. Place it on the middle rack of your preheated oven and bake for 10 minutes.

5. Fill a small saucepan with water to a depth of one inch. Then place a medium metal mixing bowl on top and turn the heat to medium-low to create a double boiler. To the mixing bowl add the egg yolks, vanilla, and Coconut Dream and begin to whisk immediately. The mixture will turn a pale yellow color and begin to froth and thicken. Do not stop whisking or the egg will cook and you'll end up with scrambled eggs.

6. When the mixture has about doubled in size add the chocolate and Earth Balance and continue to whisk. Both will gradually melt into the egg mixture. As soon as all the chocolate has melted and the batter is creamy and even in color, take the bowl off the saucepan and turn off the heat. Pour the batter directly onto the cookie crust you made earlier and smooth out the top.

7. Allow the tart to come to room temperature, then refrigerate for 3 hours to allow it to set. When you're ready to serve, run a chef's knife under hot water and dry with a tea towel, then cut the tart into approximately 1 x 1 inch squares.

Makes 16 – 20 squares

Personal Peach Cobbler

When peaches are in season this recipe really cannot be beat. Avoid the tedium of slicing peaches for a tray of crumble by simply removing the pits and using the peach as the vehicle for the crumble topping. Slow cooking leaves the flesh of the peaches gooey and caramelized and highly intensifies the flavor.

Allergen Information
This recipe does not call for any dairy, nuts, peanuts, citrus, or egg.

Tools You Will Need	**Ingredients**
Paring knife	2 – 3 large ripe peaches
Cutting board	5 tbsp Earth Balance or shortening
Medium mixing bowl	¼ cup sugar
Spatula	⅓ cup brown sugar
Spoon	2 tbsp organic honey
Parchment paper	Pinch of salt
Glass baking dish	A good handful of instant oats (about ½ cup)
	½ tsp ground cinnamon
	½ tsp ground ginger
	2 tbsp all purpose flour

Method
1. Preheat oven to 350F and line a glass baking dish with parchment paper.
2. Thoroughly pat the peaches dry after washing them. Then cut them in half and remove the pits. If they are ripe enough you should be able to twist the sides of the peach after slicing and they should easily pull apart.
3. In a mixing bowl combine Earth Balance or shortening, sugar, brown sugar, organic honey, salt, oats, cinnamon, and ginger. Once this is all combined, add the flour. It should be just enough for the mixture to begin clumping together.
4. Place the peach halves facing up in the dish. They can be clustered together and touching, not to worry.
5. Use your fingers to make little mounds of filling in the center of each peach, pressing it lightly in place. You can add a little pad of Earth Balance or shortening on top of each peach if you'd like, to help the tops sizzle.
6. Place the peaches in preheated oven and bake for about 25 minutes, until the peaches look like they're melting and caramelizing and the filling is lightly browned. These are best served warm.

Serves 4 – 6

Polka Dot Berry Pie

A fun take on a typical dessert, shortbread cookies make up the crust of this pie. I wanted to make a pie that was totally foolproof and what part of the pie is harder to mess up than the crust? By swapping it out for shortbread cutouts and a no-roll crust, this is a great pie recipe for beginners.

Allergen Information
This recipe does not call for any dairy, nuts, citrus, or peanuts.

Tools You Will Need
1 medium mixing bowl
Dinner fork
Standard pie pan
Measuring cups and spoons
Rolling pin
Parchment paper
Baking sheet
Small round cookie cutter or espresso cup
Paring knife and cutting board
Saucepan

Ingredients

Shortbread crust
$^1/_3$ cup Earth Balance or shortening or lard
1 egg yolk
$^1/_3$ cup sugar
A generous pinch of salt
1 cup all purpose flour

Berry Filling
1.25 lb fresh berries (Mix of strawberry, blueberry, raspberry, and/or blackberry)
¼ cup water
¼ cup sugar
1 tbsp honey
A pinch of salt

Polka Dot Shortbread cookie topping

⅓ cup vegan butter or shortening or lard

1 cup all purpose flour

¼ cup sugar

1 tsp honey

A pinch of salt

1 large egg

½ tsp pure vanilla extract

A pinch of cinnamon

Method

1. Preheat the oven to 400F.
2. The first step is to make the simple shortbread crust. Cream the Earth Balance or shortening and sugar using your fork in a medium mixing bowl. Make sure it is well combined and completely smooth.
3. Add the egg yolk by separating the egg. To separate an egg, crack it on the counter and then split the shell in half, making sure none of the egg comes out. Then shift all the egg into one half of the shell. Over the sink, pour the egg into the other half of the shell and let the white fall out into the sink. Do this once more so that just the yolk is left in one half of the shell. Pour it into the mixing bowl and cream together with the sugar and Earth Balance or shortening.
4. Add the salt and flour and mix together until the mixture starts to come together in little pea-sized clumps. It will be a very crumbly and dry dough that does not stick together.
5. Pour it into a standard-size pie pan and gently spread it around the bottom so that it is in an even layer. Make sure you wash your hands before doing this!
6. Then start to firmly press the dough down and up the sides of the pan. Don't press it too hard or it will start to crack.
7. Place the pie pan on a cookie sheet and pop it into the heated oven. Set your timer for 10 minutes. When the time is up the crust should be lightly golden and crispy around the edges.
8. Set it aside to cool. Meanwhile you can prepare the filling. Wash and remove the stems from 1.25 lb of berries. Use a small thin knife called a paring knife to remove the stems from strawberries, if you are using that berry. Strawberries can be cut into quarters and smaller berries can be left whole.
9. Place them in a small pot called a saucepan along with the water, honey, sugar, and salt. Turn the heat to medium and let the berries come to a simmer. You will know when it's simmering because there will be a lot of bubbles coming to the top! Then turn it to medium-low and let it simmer for about 20 – 25 minutes, stirring often.
10. While the filling is simmering you can make the polka dot shortbread crust. Using the same bowl and fork from the bottom crust, cream together the vegan butter and sugar. Then add the egg and mix well. It might be a slightly clumpy mixture but that's okay. Then add the vanilla, flour, and salt and mix until the dough comes together in big clumps.

11. Lay a sheet of parchment paper on the countertop. Pour the dough onto the paper and use your hands to form it into a ball. Then dust it with a bit of flour and use your rolling pin to roll it out to about a ¼ inch thickness. Cut circles out of the dough using either a small round cookie cutter or an espresso cup. Set the dough circles aside.

12. Turn the oven down to 350F.

13. Give the berry mixture a final stir and check that it has simmered down to half the amount you started with. Pour into the cooled pie crust and spread around evenly with a fork or spoon.

14. Lay the circles around the top of your pie in whatever pattern you want. They can even overlap each other! When you are finished decorating the top, place the pie (still on a baking sheet) into the heated oven for 15 – 20 minutes.

15. Take the pie out of the oven after 15 – 20 minutes using oven gloves and allow it to cool completely before cutting out the first slice.

The polka dot crust dough can be made up to a day ahead of time, wrapped in plastic wrap, and kept in the fridge.

Apple Pie

Cinnamon, brown sugar, and loads of apples crammed into a flaky crust.

Allergen Information
This recipe does not call for any dairy, nuts, citrus, or peanuts.

Tools You Will Need
Large mixing bowl
Standard pie pan
Measuring cups and spoons
Paring knife and cutting board
Rolling pin
Mixing spoon
Large fork
Parchment paper

Ingredients

Crust
1 cup lard
½ cup shortening
3 cups all purpose flour
²/₃ cup very cold water
¹/₃ cup sugar
1 tsp honey
A pinch of salt
1 egg for brushing (optional)

Filling
2 pounds McIntosh applies
5 tbsp demerara or dark brown sugar
Pinch of salt
1 tsp ground cinnamon
1 tbsp flour

Method:

1. The first step is to prepare the crust. To do this, add the flour, sugar, and salt to a large mixing bowl and mix until well combined. Then add the honey and vegan butter to the bowl. If using vegan butter over shortening or lard, be sure to leave it on the counter at room temperature for about 15 – 20 minutes prior to use. Use a fork or your hands to mix the ingredients together. Cut the vegan butter into small pea-sized balls.

2. Form a well in the center of the bowl and pour the water in. Then use either a large fork or a mixing spoon to fold the dry ingredients into the wet. Stop mixing when it forms a ball, and be sure not to over mix as it will toughen the dough.

3. Fold the dough ball up in parchment paper and refrigerate for 1 – 2 hours.

4. To prepare the filling, peel and core 2 pounds of McIntosh apples. McIntosh apples are perfect for pie filling because they are a really affordable variety of apple and melt down nicely without retaining any crunch. Slice the peeled and cored apples lengthwise into long, thin slices.

5. Add the apples, sugar, salt, and cinnamon to a large mixing bowl and mix it all together until the apples are well coated in sugar and spice. Set aside until the crust is ready for rolling.

6. After the dough is finished chilling in the fridge, unfold the parchment paper (it's good to store it on a piece of parchment that is large enough to roll it out on after) and lightly sprinkle with flour on all sides. At this point you can set the oven to 350F to preheat. Cut the dough in half and set one piece aside. Roll the other half out to a ¼ inch thickness and then lay it over the pie pan, pressing very lightly into the edges so it forms to the shape of the pan.

7. Give the apples a final stir to make sure they are well coated with sugar and pour them into the pie pan. It will look like a lot of apples for the size of the pan, but that's totally normal. They will shrink down significantly during the cooking process.

8. Roll the other half of the dough out to ¼ inch thickness and drape over the filling. Cut off the excess dough (both top and bottom layers), leaving a 1 inch border around the perimeter of the pie. This will give you some dough to shape into a fancy border around the edge. You can fold the edges over and crimp with a fork, or use your fingers to scallop the edges.

9. Egg wash will add a nice golden sheen to the top crust; however, it is optional and should be left out if you are accommodating an egg allergy. To prepare the egg wash, crack 1 egg into a small bowl and mix with 1 tbsp of water to thin it out, and beat well with a fork. Use a pastry brush to paint a thin layer of egg wash over the top crust, making sure to smooth out any little puddles that may form in the crevices.

10. Use a paring knife to cut a couple slits in the center of the top crust to allow for airflow.

11. Pop the pie in the oven on the middle rack and bake for 45 minutes. You can add more egg wash halfway through the baking process to add extra sheen, and you can even add a sprinkle of sugar for extra crunch.

12. When finished baking, remove the pie and allow to cool for 2 hours so the filling can firm up, and then slice and serve.

Peach Pineapple Crumble

When I came up with this recipe I was looking to improve on an existing favorite, peach crumble, by making it new and unique. After many semi-improvements, I realized that simply roasting fruit is the best way to add flavor, and so adding roasted pineapple chunks became the solution.

Allergen Information
This recipe does not call for any dairy, nuts, peanuts, citrus, or egg.

Tools You Will Need
Measuring cups and spoons
Baking sheet
Parchment paper
Baking dish
Large mixing bowl
Paring knife and cutting board
Peeler
Large fork
Mixing spoon

Ingredients
Filling
3 tbsp sugar
4 – 5 cups sliced ripe peaches

Crumble
½ cup vegan butter or shortening
½ cup brown sugar
¼ cup sugar
¼ cup oats
½ cup flour
Pinch of salt

Method
 1. Preheat oven to 400F.
 2. Begin by preparing the fruit for the crumble filling. First, wash and pat dry the peaches and then cut them into segments about ¼ inch wide. The width of the peaches doesn't have to be exact, as the filling will all bake down anyways. Just aim to make them all relatively the same size. This is much easier with free stone peaches.

179

3. You can either buy a pineapple already cored (which I highly recommend as a time saver) or you can peel the pineapple yourself. Make sure your knife is quite sharp, and begin by chopping off the top. Then cut it downwards into quarters so you have 4 wedges. Lay each wedge on its side, and slide out the core. If you are unsure where the core ends, it is usually a bit lighter in color and has a woody texture. Once the cores are removed, slide your knife along the bottom of the pineapple (still laying on its side) between the skin and the flesh. This is where having a sharp knife is really important. Always be sure to cut away from your body. In one long motion you should slice the skin off the flesh of the pineapple. Then cut it up into smaller pieces for baking.

4. This step is optional; however, it adds loads of flavor and improved texture to the crumble. Roast the pineapple by first laying the pieces out on a baking sheet lined with parchment paper, and then pop it into the preheated oven for about 25 minutes, until the fruit is golden brown around the edges. You'll notice that it has dried out a bit and no longer looks watery, but don't worry because it's still very juicy on the inside.

5. Lower the oven to 350F.

6. In a large bowl combine the peaches, pineapple, and 3 tablespoons of sugar. Mix well and then pour it all out into a baking dish.

7. Mash the vegan butter or shortening together in a large bowl with the sugars until fluffy. Then add the flour, salt, and oats and mix well. It should come together in clumps but not form a ball. You can add cinnamon, honey, or ground ginger for an added kick.

8. Pour the clumpy crumble mixture over the fruit and distribute it somewhat evenly.

9. Place the baking dish in the oven on the middle rack and let it bake for at least 25 minutes, until the top is golden and the filling is syrupy and starting to bubble up through the crust.

10. Once it's finished baking, leave it to cool for at least 30 minutes. It is best served warm.

Maple Berry Pie

Most people think to pair maple syrup with apples; however, blueberries and maple syrup are truly a match made in heaven. The warmth and thickness of the syrup makes it a great accompaniment to tart fresh berries.

Allergen Information
This recipe does not call for any dairy, nuts, peanuts, citrus, or egg.

Tools You Will Need
Large mixing bowl
Measuring cups and spoons
Rolling pin
Parchment paper
Large fork
Paring knife
Mixing spoon

Ingredients

Crust
¼ cup shortening
½ cup lard
1 ½ cups all purpose flour
¹/₃ cup very cold water
1 tbsp sugar
1 tsp honey
A generous pinch of salt

Filling
2 pints blueberries
1 pint raspberries
1 pint strawberries
¹/₃ cup maple syrup
½ tsp pure vanilla extract
½ tsp ground cinnamon
½ tsp ground ginger

Method

1. Add all of the filling ingredients to a medium pot and turn to medium-low heat. Stir well, so that all the berries are coated with maple syrup and sugar. Avoid using blackberries because they release a lot of water and will compromise the texture of the pie filling.

2. When the berries come to a low boil, turn the heat down to low and let them simmer for about 40 – 50 minutes, until they have reduced and have a syrupy consistency.

3. While the filling is simmering you can prepare the crust. In a large mixing bowl, combine the shortening, lard, flour, sugar, and salt. The best way to combine the ingredients is to "cut" them in using a large fork. The vegan butter should be cut down to the size of small peas.

4. Make a well in the center of the dry ingredients and add in the water and honey at once. Then use a spatula or fork to gradually pull the dry ingredients into the center. The mixture should come together into a ball. Turn this ball out onto a large piece of parchment paper sprinkled with flour. Use your hands to pat it smooth and then flatten it into a disk. Wrap it up in the parchment paper and put it in the fridge until the pie is ready to assemble.

5. When the berries have finished simmering, turn the stove off and move them off the heat. It is time to roll out the pie crust and preheat the oven to 375F. Open the parchment paper and sprinkle flour over the dough on both sides. Then take a rolling pin and roll the dough out to a ¼ inch thickness. The pattern for the top crust will be a crosshatch, like a picnic basket. Drape the dough over the pie pan and press it into the edges so there are no air pockets. Use a paring knife to trim off the excess dough, leaving about a half inch rim of dough around the pan.

6. Press the remaining scraps of dough into a ball and dust with flour again. Place the dough on the parchment paper and roll it out again into a ¼ inch thickness. Try to form it into a large rectangle. Cut the rectangle into strips about ½ an inch in thickness. You should end up with 6 – 8 strips.

7. Pour the pie filling into the pan lined with pastry and smooth out the top. Then lay half of the strips of crust across the top of the pie. They should all be going in the same direction and should be evenly spread out across the top of the filling. Take the remaining strips and begin laying them one by one across the pie in the other direction. To create a true crosshatch pattern, be sure to slip them under, over, then under the strips going in the opposite direction. When you move on to the next strip, overlap it in the opposite way (over, under, over). You can always readjust as many times as needed, but try not to let the pastry warm up too much or it won't cook properly.

8. Fold the excess pie crust around the rim of the pan up over the edges and use your fingers to press it into place.

9. Put the pie in the center rack of the oven and bake for about 20 – 30 minutes, until the crust is golden brown.

10. Leave the pie to chill for several hours to give the filling a chance to firm up again.

Spicy Apple Raisin Pie

Apple pie is given a little twist by the addition of raisins, maple syrup, and spices.

Allergen Information
This recipe does not call for any dairy, nuts, citrus, or peanuts.

Tools You Will Need
Large mixing bowl
Paring knife
Cutting board
Parchment paper
Rolling pin
Large fork
Mixing spoon
Measuring cups and spoons

Ingredients

Crust
1 ½ cups vegan butter or shortening or lard
3 cups all purpose flour
²/₃ cup very cold water
¹/₃ cup sugar
A generous pinch of salt
1 egg for brushing (optional)

Filling
2 pounds McIntosh apples
2 tbsp demerara or dark brown sugar
Pinch of salt
1 tsp ground cinnamon
½ tsp ground cloves
1 tsp ground ginger
2 tbsp maple syrup
1 tbsp flour
A handful of raisins

Method

1. In a large mixing bowl, combine the vegan butter, flour, sugar, and salt. The best way to combine the ingredients is to "cut" them in using a large fork. The vegan butter should be cut down to the size of small peas.

2. Make a well in the center of the dry ingredients and add in the water. Then use a spatula or fork to gradually pull the dry ingredients into the center. The mixture should come together into a ball. Turn this ball out onto a large piece of parchment paper sprinkled with flour. Use your hands to pat it smooth and then flatten it into a disk. Wrap it up in the parchment paper and allow it to rest in the fridge for at least an hour.

3. While the crust is resting you can prepare the filling. Peel and core 2 pounds of McIntosh apples and cut into thin slices using a paring knife. Add them to a large mixing bowl and toss with the sugar, salt, spices, flour, maple syrup, and raisins so that everything is well coated. The filling can sit aside at room temperature until the dough is finished resting.

4. When the dough is finished resting, it is time to roll out the pie crust and preheat the oven to 375F. Open the parchment paper and sprinkle flour over the dough on both sides. Then take a rolling pin and roll the dough out to a ¼ inch thickness. Cut it in half and drape one half over the pie pan and press it into the edges so there are no air pockets. Use a paring knife to trim off the excess dough, leaving about a half inch rim of dough around the pan.

5. Pour the filling into the bottom crust and spread it out evenly.

6. Press the remaining scraps of dough into a ball and dust with flour again. Place the dough on the parchment paper and roll it out again into a ¼ inch thickness. Drape the dough over the filling and use a paring knife to cut off the excess, leaving about an inch around the perimeter. You can either crimp the dough with a fork or with your fingers to create a nice border. Use a knife to pierce a few slits in the center of the top crust.

7. Egg wash is optional; however, it gives the crust a nice glossy finish. To make egg wash, beat one egg with 1 tbsp of water and brush it over the crust using a pastry brush.

8. Bake for 30 – 40 minutes and allow to cool for a minimum of 2 hours before slicing.

Serves 8 – 10

Personal Apple Crumble

Allergen Information
This recipe does not call for any dairy, nuts, peanuts, citrus, or egg.

Tools You Will Need
Paring knife
Cutting board
Medium mixing bowl
Spatula
Spoon
Parchment paper
Glass baking dish

Ingredients
2 – 3 large McIntosh apples
5 tbsp Earth Balance or shortening
$^1/_4$ cup sugar
$^1/_3$ cup brown sugar
2 tbsp organic honey
Pinch of salt
A good handful of instant oats (about ½ cup)
½ tsp ground cinnamon
½ tsp ground ginger
2 tbsp all purpose flour

Method
1. Preheat oven to 350 and line a glass baking dish with parchment paper.
2. Cut the apples in half and remove the stem, core, and seeds. Before slicing them in half you can use an apple core remover to make this easier if you are not very confident with a paring knife.
3. In a mixing bowl combine Earth Balance or shortening, sugar, brown sugar, organic honey, salt, oats, cinnamon, and ginger. Once this is all combined add the flour. It should be just enough for the mixture to begin clumping together.
4. Place the apple halves facing up in the dish. They can be clustered together and touching, not to worry.
5. Use your fingers to make little mounds of filling in the center of each apple, pressing it lightly in place. You can add a little pad of Earth Balance or shortening on top of each apple if you'd like, to help the tops sizzle.
6. Place the apples in preheated oven and bake for about 25 minutes, until they look like they're melting and caramelizing and the filling is lightly browned. These are best served warm.

Serves 4 – 6

✤ EGG-FREE CUPCAKES

Replacing egg in baked goods can be very challenging because it's difficult to know what amounts and which ingredients to use for the best substitution. This chapter contains a recipe for basic egg-free cupcakes, which is then altered to make 6 additional egg-free recipes. Once you've mastered one recipe, you've mastered all seven! Even if you do not have to accommodate an egg allergy, I strongly encourage you to try baking without eggs. The texture difference is minimal and the flavor just as delicious as traditional cake recipes.

Basic Egg-Free Vanilla Cake

Read over this first basic recipe – then see how it can be varied to create more interesting cupcake creations. Use this recipe as the base for each of the recipes in this chapter.

Allergen information
This recipe does not call for any dairy, nuts, peanuts, or egg.

Tools You Will Need	Ingredients	
A medium-sized mixing bowl	¾ cup vegetable oil	1 ½ tbsp of lemon juice (any citrus will do)
A fork or whisk	½ cup water	1 ½ cups all purpose flour
Measuring spoons and cups	1 cup of plain, unsweetened applesauce	½ cup powdered sugar
Muffin pan (or a mini muffin pan)		1 ½ tsp baking soda
Paper muffin cups	½ tsp pure vanilla extract	1 tsp baking powder

*In any of the recipes in this chapter, water can be replaced with coconut milk, flax milk, rice milk, or fruit juice, so long as the ingredient list of that particular product does not list any form of dairy, nuts, peanuts, legumes, or citrus.

Method
1. Preheat your oven to 375F.
2. Line muffin tin with muffin cups. This recipe will make 25 – 30 medium cupcakes, or 40 – 48 mini cupcakes.
3. Add oil, water, applesauce, lemon juice, and pure vanilla extract to a medium mixing bowl. Combine well using a fork or whisk.
4. Add flour, sugar, baking soda, and baking powder, to the wet ingredients all at once. Mix until just combined – make sure you do not over mix!
5. Spoon batter into lined muffin cups, about ¾ full.
6. Place in preheated 375F oven.
7. For medium cupcakes: bake for 18 – 22 minutes, until toothpick inserted in center comes out clean. For mini cupcakes: bake for 8 – 10 minutes, until toothpick inserted in center comes out clean.
8. Once removed from the oven, leave in the pan until they are cool enough to touch. Transfer to a paper towel, tea towel, or cooling rack, until they come to room temperature.
9. While they are cooling you can prepare the Basic Frosting recipe on page 267. To ice in a basic star design, load frosting into a piping bag with a medium star tip. Touch the tip to the cupcake top and begin moving it around the edge of the cake in a circular motion until you reach the center.

Makes 12 large cupcakes or 18 – 20 medium cupcakes or 35 – 40 mini cupcakes

Watermelon Cupcakes

A simple way to add some summery whimsy to basic vanilla cupcakes, this vanilla cake is pink on the inside with chocolate chips acting as the seeds and green frosting as the skin. Kids will love this cute take on vanilla cupcakes.

Allergen information

This recipe does not call for any egg, dairy, nuts, or peanuts.

Tools You Will Need	Ingredients	
A medium-sized mixing bowl	¾ cup vegetable oil	1 ½ cups all purpose flour
A small mixing bowl	½ cup water	½ cup powdered sugar
A fork or whisk	1 cup of plain, unsweetened	1 ½ tsp baking soda
Measuring spoons and cups	applesauce	1 tsp baking powder
Muffin pan (or a mini muffin pan)	½ tsp pure vanilla extract	5 drops of red food coloring
Paper muffin cups	1 ½ tbsp of lemon juice (any citrus will do)	5 drops of green food coloring
		⅓ to ½ cup of chocolate chips (preferably mini chocolate chips)

*There are many brands of allergy friendly chocolate chips that are free of the most common allergens. It may require a trip to a health food store to find them.

Method

1. Preheat oven to 375F and line muffin pan with paper liners.
2. In a small mixing bowl toss the chocolate chips with 1 tbsp of flour so that all the chips are lightly coated. Set aside for later.
3. Combine oil, water, applesauce, lemon juice, and vanilla in a medium mixing bowl. Add flour, sugar, baking powder, baking soda, and red food coloring all at once. Mix until just combined.
4. Add the chocolate chips coated in flour and fold them in using your fork. Be sure not to over mix the batter at this stage. The chocolate chips should just be fairly well distributed throughout the batter.
6. Spoon into muffin cups and bake for 18 – 22 minutes (for medium to large cupcakes) or 8 – 10 minutes (for mini cupcakes).
7. When cupcakes are cool enough to touch, place them on a paper towel or tea towel until they come to room temperature.
8. While cupcakes are cooling, prepare Basic Vanilla Frosting recipe found on page 267. Add 5 drops of green food coloring to the frosting and mix well.
9. Spread frosting on cupcakes with a knife for a homestyle look. Or spoon frosting into a piping bag with a round tip and pipe it in a circle around the top of the cupcake unti you reach the center.

Makes 12 large cupcakes or 18 – 20 medium cupcakes or 35 – 40 mini cupcakes

Sandy Beaches

A sure fire hit for summertime, these cute cupcakes are topped with fake sand made from brown sugar and crumbled graham crackers, and flavored like the tropics with strawberry and coconut cake. Finished off with a cocktail umbrella they're a little slice of paradise.

Allergen information
This recipe does not call for any dairy, nuts, peanuts, or egg.

Tools You Will Need
A medium-sized mixing bowl
A small mixing bowl
A fork or whisk
Measuring spoons and cups
Muffin pan (or a mini muffin pan)
Paper muffin cups
Cutting board and knife
Rolling pin
Plastic freezer bag
Toothpick umbrellas

Ingredients
¾ cup vegetable oil
½ cup water
1 cup of plain, unsweetened applesauce
½ tsp pure vanilla extract
1 ½ tbsp of lemon juice (any citrus will do)
1 ½ cups all purpose flour
½ cup powdered sugar
1 ½ tsp baking soda
1 tsp baking powder

1 pint of strawberries
¼ cup shredded, unsweetened coconut
20 graham crackers
3 tbsp brown sugar or light brown sugar
¾ cup confectioner's sugar
1 tbsp water

Method

1. Preheat oven to 375F and line muffin pan with paper muffin cups.

2. Wash strawberries and remove the stems. Then, dice them into cubes about ¼ inch wide. Set them aside for later.

3. In a medium mixing bowl, combine oil, applesauce, water, lemon juice, and vanilla using a fork.

4. Add the flour, sugar, baking powder, and baking soda all at once and mix until just combined. Fold in the strawberries and coconut so that they are evenly distributed throughout the batter.

5. Spoon into muffin cups and place in preheated 375F oven. Bake for 18 – 22 minutes (for medium to large cupcakes) or 8 – 10 minutes (for mini muffins). They are done when toothpick inserted in center comes out clean.

6. While cupcakes are baking, in a small mixing bowl combine 1 tbsp of water and ¾ cup of confectioner's sugar until it forms a paste. If it is too thick, you can add a quarter tsp of water at a time until it is loose enough to stir.

7. Then take the graham crackers and put them in a freezer strength plastic zipper bag and seal the top, making sure all the air is let out. Use a marble or wood rolling pin to gently break up the crackers until they are powder. Some occasional small chunks are okay. If there are too many chunks or if the chunks are too large, they will not stick to the top of the cupcakes. Set the crunched crackers aside for later.

8. Once you have removed cupcakes from the oven, let them cool in the tray until they are cool enough to touch. Then transfer them to a tea towel or paper towel to cool completely.

9. When they are cooled completely, dip the tops of the cupcakes one by one into the confectioner's sugar mixture and then into the graham cracker crumbs. Sprinkle some brown sugar over the tops to create a bit more texture and make it look like real sand.

10. To complete the beach effect, stick a toothpick umbrella in each of the cupcakes off to the side and with the umbrella open.

11. If you have extra time and you want to get really creative you can prepare a quarter of the basic frosting recipe on page 267. Dye it orange with 3 drops of red food coloring and 5 drops of yellow food coloring. Scoop the frosting into a pastry bag with a fine round tip. To create a small crab walking along the beach, ice an oval about ¾ inch wide. Then ice 2 small lines extending from the crab for legs. Finally, ice 1 bent line on either side of the crab for claws.

Makes 12 large cupcakes or 18 – 20 medium cupcakes or 35 – 40 mini cupcakes

Strawberry Sundae (with a cherry on top)

These cupcakes are for those kids who crave decadent desserts. A vanilla cupcake is filled with a real strawberry center, then topped with frosting reminiscent of whipped cream and a maraschino cherry. Oh and they're also drizzled with melted chocolate just like the chocolate sauce that adorns the peaks of a sundae. Yep, these will impress any classroom of kids.

Allergen information
This recipe does not call for any dairy, nuts, peanuts, or egg.

Tools You Will Need
A medium-sized mixing bowl
A small mixing bowl
A fork or whisk
Measuring spoons and cups
Muffin pan (or a mini muffin pan)
Paper muffin cups
2 small saucepans and a spoon
Small plastic zipper bag

Ingredients
¾ cup vegetable oil
½ cup water
1 cup of plain, unsweetened applesauce
½ tsp pure vanilla extract
1 ½ tbsp of lemon juice (any citrus will do)
1 ½ cups all purpose flour
½ cup powdered sugar
1 ½ tsp baking soda
1 tsp baking powder

1 pint of strawberries
2 tbsp confectioner's sugar
Maraschino cherries
½ cup Enjoy Life chocolate chips

Method

1. This first part should be done ahead of time – at least an hour – but the farther ahead of time you can do it, the better. Wash and remove the stems from a pint of strawberries, then cut them into quarters. Place them in a small saucepan with 2 tbsp of confectioner's sugar and a tsp of water. Mix them well and turn the heat on to low. Let them simmer, stirring often to prevent sticking to the pot. When they are thickened and the berries are soft in texture (after about 20 minutes), remove them from heat and transfer to a small bowl.

2. Let them stand until they have reached room temperature, then place in the fridge until fully cooled. Once cooled, they will no longer be runny and will have a firmer texture. If you are in a hurry you can use prepared strawberry jam to supplement the homemade jam. Just make sure it is well chilled, real strawberry jam.

3. Preheat oven to 375F and line muffin pan with paper muffin cups.

4. In a medium bowl combine the oil, applesauce, lemon juice, water, and vanilla until well combined.

5. Add the flour, baking powder, baking soda, and sugar, stirring until just combined.

6. Fill each muffin cup halfway up with batter. Then, scoop a dollop of your cold strawberry mixture into the center of that batter, making sure that there is a rim of batter around all the edges. For a medium to large muffin cup, this will be about a tbsp of strawberry. For a mini muffin cup it will be about a tsp.

7. Then spoon more batter on top of the strawberry mixture in each cup, until they are about ¾ full.

8. Place in a preheated oven and bake for 8 – 10 minutes for mini muffins, 18 – 22 minutes for medium to large cupcakes.

9. When they are done they will be a golden color and a toothpick inserted into the cake will come out clean.

10. Let them cool in the pan until they are cool enough to touch, then transfer them to a paper towel or tea towel to cool completely.

11. For the topping, prepare one batch of the Basic Frosting Recipe found on page 267. Load the frosting into a piping bag with a star tip, and pipe a swirl on each cupcake, starting in the center. Try to make the swirl tall and thin, like an ice cream cone.

12. For the chocolate drizzle, melt the chocolate chips either on the stove or in the microwave. If you use the microwave the bowl will be very hot, so make sure you get an adult to help you take it out. Then stir the chocolate well to melt all the chunks. To melt it on the stove, place the chocolate chips in a small saucepan and turn to medium-low heat. Stir it constantly with a spoon until all the chocolate is melted. Then turn the heat off right away.

13. When chocolate is melted, load it into a small plastic zipper bag and seal the top. Use scissors to cut a small bit of the tip off to make it like a piping bag. Then drizzle it all over the vanilla frosting. The messier, the better! It doesn't have to look perfect.

14. Place one maraschino cherry on top of each cupcake while the frosting and chocolate are still warm and soft. Then put them in the fridge right away to harden.

Makes 12 large cupcakes or 18 – 20 medium cupcakes or 35 – 40 mini cupcakes

Tie-Dye Dude

For the psychedelic surfer dude in your home bake up a batch of these hippie dippie cupcakes. Mixing together different colors of batter these cupcakes are a true tie-dye creation.

Allergen Information
This recipe does not call for any egg, dairy, nuts, or peanuts.

Tools You Will Need
A medium-sized mixing bowl
Several small mixing bowls
A fork or whisk
Measuring spoons and cups
Muffin pan (or a mini muffin pan)
Paper muffin cups

Ingredients
¾ cup vegetable oil
½ cup water
1 cup of plain, unsweetened applesauce
½ tsp pure vanilla extract
1 ½ tbsp of lemon juice (any citrus will do)
1 ½ cups all purpose flour
½ cup powdered sugar
1 ½ tsp baking soda
1 tsp baking powder
Several different food colors (as many as you like, but 3 or 4 should suffice)

Method
1. Prepare the Basic Egg-Free Vanilla Cupcake batter recipe as outlined on page 193; steps 1 – 4.
2. Divide the cake batter evenly into separate bowls – the same number of bowls as colors of food coloring.
3. Place a few drops of food coloring in each bowl until the color is as bright as you like. If you add 3 – 5 drops of food color to a bowl, it will be a light pastel color. If you add 6 – 10 drops of food color to a bowl, it will be a brighter color.
4. Mix the food color into the batter until it is evenly mixed through.
5. Scoop one spoon of the first batter color into the bottom of each muffin cup. Then take the second color and scoop one spoon of it into each muffin cup. Continue doing this for each color you prepared until all the batter is in the muffin cups. This will create a striped/layered color look.

6. If you want the cupcakes to look like real tie-dye, take a toothpick and stick it in the center of the batter in each muffin cup. Then swirl it around to mix the colors together. Swirl it in a circle about five to seven times, and then remove the toothpick.

7. Place muffin pans in your preheated oven and bake for 18 – 22 minutes (for medium or large cupcakes) or 8 – 10 minutes (for mini cupcakes). They are finished cooking when a toothpick inserted comes out clean.

8. Once removed from the oven, leave in the pan until they are cool enough to touch. Transfer to a paper towel, tea towel, or cooling rack, until they come to room temperature.

9. Prepare the Basic Vanilla Frosting recipe on page 267 and divide it into 3 or 4 separate bowls. Put 3 drops of red food color in the first bowl, 3 drops of blue food color in the second bowl, 3 drops of yellow food color in the third bowl, and 3 drops of green food color in the fourth bowl. You can use whichever food colors you prefer. Mix the food colorings into the plain vanilla confectioner's until the color is completely blended through.

10. Prepare a pastry bag with a star shaped tip.

11. Scoop one heaping tablespoon of each color into the bag, alternating between colors until all the confectioner's is in the pastry bag.

12. Place the tip on the edge of the cupcake and rotate it in a circle around the edge of the cupcake until you reach the center to create a classic swirl design. The result will be a stripey multicolored icing effect.

Makes 12 large cupcakes or 18 – 20 medium cupcakes or 35 – 40 mini cupcakes

Canada Day Cupcakes

Red and white cupcakes with maple sugar on top. I have such fond memories of eating maple sugar straight from the maple syrup festivals in Northern Ontario that my aunt and uncle would bring me every year. Anything maple makes a festive addition to a Canadian-themed treat.

Allergen information
This recipe does not call for any egg, dairy, nuts, or peanuts.

Tools You Will Need
2 medium mixing bowls
A fork or whisk
Measuring spoons and cups
A muffin pan (or a mini muffin pan)
Paper muffin cups

Ingredients
¾ cup vegetable oil
½ cup water
1 cup of plain, unsweetened applesauce
½ tsp pure vanilla extract
1 ½ tbsp of lemon juice (any citrus will do)
1 ½ cups all purpose flour
½ cup powdered sugar
1 ½ tsp baking soda
1 tsp baking powder
15 – 20 drops of red food coloring
Maple sugar candies – 24 pieces for large cupcakes, 25 – 30 for medium cupcakes, or 40 – 48 for mini cupcakes

Method
1. Preheat oven to 375F and line muffin pan or mini muffin pan with muffin cups.
2. Prepare the Basic Egg-Free Vanilla Cupcake recipe on found on page 193, steps 1 – 4.
3. Divide the batter into two bowls. Add 15 – 20 drops of red food coloring to one of the bowls, and mix until it is completely blended through.
4. For medium or large cupcakes, scoop one tablespoon of white batter into each muffin cup. Then scoop one tablespoon of red batter into each muffin cup. Continue alternating colors of batter until the cups are filled ¾ way full. The finished product will look like red and white stripes, resembling the Canadian flag.
5. Place in preheated 375F oven and bake for 18 – 22 minutes, until toothpick inserted in center comes out clean.
6. Once removed from the oven, leave in the pan until they are cool enough to touch. Transfer to a paper towel, tea towel, or cooling rack, until they come to room temperature.
7. Prepare Basic Vanilla Frosting recipe on page 267. Scoop it into a piping bag with whatever shape tip you prefer. Do a basic swirl design in the center of the cupcake and top with a maple sugar candy. If you do not have maple sugar candies, you can do a drizzle of maple syrup instead.

Makes 12 large cupcakes or 18 – 20 medium cupcakes or 35 – 40 mini cupcakes

Abominable Snowmen

With coconut and brown sugar making these cupcakes light as snow, they are yummy treats for a winter party. The tops are decorated with shredded coconut and frosting to make them look like frightful (or jolly) snowmen. I think they make a great snow day activity.

Allergen information
This recipe does not call for any egg, dairy, nuts, or peanuts.

Tools You Will Need
Medium mixing bowl
2 small mixing bowls
A fork or whisk
Measuring spoons and cups
A muffin pan (or a mini muffin pan)
Paper muffin cups
2 plastic freezer bags

Ingredients
¾ cup vegetable oil
½ cup water
1 cup of plain, unsweetened applesauce
½ tsp pure vanilla extract
1 ½ tbsp of lemon juice (any citrus will do)
1 ½ cups all purpose flour
½ cup powdered sugar
1 ½ tsp baking soda
1 tsp baking powder
¼ cup shredded, unsweetened coconut flakes
¼ cup demerara sugar (or dark brown sugar)

Topping
Basic frosting recipe found on page 267
5 drops black food coloring
1 drop red food coloring and 3 drops of red food coloring (or 3 drops of orange dye)
1 cup shredded coconut

Method

1. Preheat oven to 375F and line medium muffin pan with muffin cups.

2. Prepare the Basic Egg-Free Vanilla Cupcake recipe on found on page 193, steps 1-4.

3. Add coconut flakes and demerara sugar to the mixing bowl and fold it in until it is streaked throughout the batter.

4. Spoon into muffin cups until ¾ of the way full.

5. Place in preheated 375F oven and bake for 18 – 22 minutes, until toothpick inserted comes out clean and tops are golden.

6. Leave the cupcakes in the muffin pan until they are cool enough to touch. Then place them on a paper towel or tea towel to cool. The bottoms may be slightly oily due to the natural oils in the coconut that are released while baking.

7. While the cupcakes cool, prepare the Basic Vanilla Frosting recipe on page 267. Remove ½ cup of frosting and place it in a small mixing bowl. Add a couple drops of black food coloring and mix well. Then take ½ of the basic frosting and place it in a separate mixing bowl. Add either 3 drops of orange food coloring or 1 drop of red food coloring and 3 drops of yellow food coloring and mix until well combined.

8. Spread a thin layer of the basic vanilla frosting on each cupcake and immediately dip into the coconut flakes. Press lightly on the coconut to make sure it sticks to the frosting.

9. Scoop the orange frosting into a plastic freezer bag and snip off the tip to make a very small opening. Using this as a piping bag, pipe a long triangle in the center of each cupcake to create a carrot-like nose.

10. Scoop the black confectioner's into a plastic freezer bag and snip off the tip to create a small opening. Using this as a piping bag, pipe 2 dots above the nose for eyes, and several dots around the bottom for a mouth. You can get creative and pipe angry eyes and eyebrows to make the snowmen abominable!

Makes 12 large cupcakes or 18 – 20 medium cupcakes or 35 – 40 mini cupcakes

CLASSIC VANILLA CAKE

Just as with the egg-free chapter, this chapter presents you with one basic cupcake recipe which is then modified to make a whole slew of different cupcakes with funky frosting and presentation. My favorite recipe from this chapter is berry shortcakes. They're so delicate and simple, but pack a punch of flavor with fresh fruit and meringue in place of whipped cream.

Classic Vanilla Cupcakes

You probably know it as the common birthday cake – and it's always a hit!

Read over this first basic recipe – then see how it can be varied to create more interesting cupcake creations.

Allergy Information
This recipe does not call for any dairy, nuts, peanuts, or citrus.

Tools You Will Need
A fork or whisk
A medium mixing bowl
Measuring cups and spoons
Muffin pan
Paper muffin cups

Ingredients
½ cup vegetable oil
3 large eggs
2 tsp pure vanilla extract
¾ cup of water
1 ½ cups all purpose flour
A pinch of salt
1 tsp baking soda
2 tsp baking powder
¾ cup sugar

Method
1. Preheat oven to 375F and line muffin tin with paper muffin cups.
2. In a medium mixing bowl, combine eggs, oil, water, and vanilla. Beat well with a fork.
3. Add the flour, salt, baking soda, baking powder, and sugar all at once. Mix with a fork until well combined, with a smooth consistency throughout.
4. Spoon into lined muffin tin and place in preheated oven. Bake for 8 – 10 minutes (for mini cupcakes) or 18 – 22 minutes (for medium to large cupcakes).
5. The cupcakes are done when a toothpick inserted in the center comes out clean. They will have a slight golden color on top.
6. Leave them in the muffin tin until they are cool enough to touch. Then transfer them to a paper towel or tea towel to cool completely.
7. To ice them, prepare a batch of Basic Vanilla Frosting, found on page 267, and ice them to your liking. Using a butter knife to slather the icing around in rough peaks will give it a nice home-style touch.

Makes 12 large cupcakes or 35 – 40 mini cupcakes

Berry Shortcakes

Classic vanilla cupcakes are split in half and stuffed with fresh strawberries and meringue like strawberry shortcake. I recommend this recipe for kids who prefer the cake over the frosting at dessert time, or who are not especially drawn to very sweet desserts. This recipe can be scaled up to a full-size cake by baking in an 8 inch round cake pan and then split in half and filled just the same way the recipe dictates for cupcakes.

Allergy Information
This recipe does not call for any dairy, nuts, peanuts, or citrus.

Tools You Will Need
A fork
A medium mixing bowl
A medium metal mixing bowl
Electric mixer with whisk attachment
Measuring cups and spoons

A knife and cutting board
Muffin pan
Paper muffin cups

Ingredients
½ cup vegetable oil
3 large eggs
2 tsp pure vanilla extract
¾ cup of water
1 ½ cups all purpose flour

A pinch of salt
1 tsp baking soda
2 tsp baking powder
¾ cup sugar

6 egg whites
½ tsp cream of tartar (optional)
1 pint of strawberries (or whichever berry you prefer)
1 tbsp powdered sugar

Method

1. Preheat oven to 375F and line muffin tin with paper muffin cups.
2. In a medium mixing bowl, combine eggs, oil, water, and vanilla. Beat well with a fork.
3. Add the flour, salt, baking soda, baking powder, and sugar all at once. Mix with a fork until well combined, with a smooth consistency throughout.
4. Spoon into lined muffin tin and place in preheated oven. Bake for 8 – 10 minutes (for mini cupcakes) or 18 – 22 minutes (for medium to large cupcakes).
5. The cupcakes are done when a toothpick inserted in the center comes out clean. They will have a slight golden color on top.
6. While the cupcakes are cooling, you can begin to prepare the filling. Wash the berries and remove any stems. Then slice them into thin slices. If you are using another kind of berry, you can leave them whole.
7. Add the egg whites and cream of tartar to your metal mixing bowl. Using an electric mixer on medium-high with a whisk attachment beat them until they form stiff peaks. Then beat in the powdered sugar until it is just combined. Keep the meringue in the fridge until the cupcakes are cooled completely.
8. When cupcakes have cooled completely, remove them from the pan and pull off the paper muffin liners.
9. Use a knife to split the cupcakes in half, removing the top from the bottom.
10. Spoon a dollop of meringue on to each of the bottom halves. Then layer berries on top. Add a bit of meringue on top of the berries if you have any left over. Then place the top half of each cupcake on top like a sandwich.

Makes 12 large cupcakes or 35 – 40 mini cupcakes

Campfire Snacks

Campfire snacks are the perfect cupcakes to make for a cottage party or barbeque in the summer. Just like s'mores, they combine the universally pleasing flavors of graham crackers, marshmallow, and chocolate.

Allergy Information

This recipe does not call for any dairy, nuts, peanuts, or citrus.

Tools You Will Need

A fork or whisk

A medium mixing bowl

Measuring cups and spoons

Muffin pan

Paper muffin cups

Chopping board and knife

Ingredients

½ cup vegetable oil

3 large eggs

2 tsp pure vanilla extract

¾ cup of water

1 ½ cups all purpose flour

A pinch of salt

1 tsp baking soda

2 tsp baking powder

¾ cup sugar

200g of mini marshmallows

18 graham crackers

Optional: replace ¼ cup of flour with ¼ cup of sifted cocoa powder to make a chocolatey cupcake

Method

1. Preheat oven to 375F and line muffin tin with paper muffin cups.
2. In a medium mixing bowl, combine eggs, oil, water, and vanilla. Beat well with a fork.
3. Add the flour, salt, baking soda, baking powder, and sugar all at once. Mix with a fork until well combined, with a smooth consistency throughout.
4. Using a spoon, fill the muffin cups halfway. Then place in preheated oven. Bake for 5 – 7 minutes (for mini cupcakes) or 8 – 10 minutes (for medium or large cupcakes).
5. The cupcakes are done when a toothpick inserted in the center comes out clean. They will have a slight golden color on top.
6. Leave them in the muffin tin until they are cool enough to touch. Then fill the remaining half of the muffin cup with a single layer of mini marshmallows. Do not pack them in too tightly, or they will overflow and stick to the muffin cup.
7. Turn the oven off and turn on the broiler.
8. Place the cupcakes under the broiler for 25 seconds (for mini size cupcakes) up to 1 minute and 15 seconds (for a larger size cupcake). Peek at them through the oven window to make sure they are not burning.
9. Meanwhile, chop the graham crackers up roughly and set them aside.
10. When you take the cupcakes out of the oven, immediately sprinkle the tops with the chopped graham cracker pieces. But make sure you don't touch the pan because it will be very hot!

Makes 18 – 20 large cupcakes or 24 – 30 medium cupcakes or 40+ mini cupcakes (good for larger groups)

*If you're pressed for time but want to spice up classic vanilla cake, you can add 2 tbsp of sprinkles to the **Classic Yellow Cake** batter recipe and icing to create confetti cakes!

Pink Lemonade Cupcakes

Almost all of my childhood summertime memories involve my mom pouring cool glasses of pink lemonade for my brother and me. In my mind it's the staple drink of summer so I decided to combine it with a cupcake to create the perfect summer dessert. These cupcakes are flavored with lemon and raspberry and decorated with frosting and a cute bendy straw to look like a glass of lemonade.

Allergy Information
This recipe does not call for any dairy, nuts, or peanuts.

Tools You Will Need
A fork or whisk
A medium mixing bowl
Measuring cups and spoons
Muffin pan
Paper muffin cups
Chopping board and knife
Citrus zester
12 bendy straws
A pair of scissors

Ingredients
½ cup vegetable oil
3 large eggs
2 tsp pure vanilla extract
¾ cup of water
1 ½ cups all purpose flour
A pinch of salt
1 tsp baking soda
2 tsp baking powder
¾ cup sugar

1 pint of raspberries
5 drops red food coloring
Finely grated zest of half a lemon

Method

1. Preheat oven to 375F and line muffin tin with paper muffin cups.
2. In a medium mixing bowl, combine eggs, oil, water, and vanilla. Beat well with a fork.
3. Add the flour, salt, baking soda, baking powder, and sugar all at once. Mix with a fork until well combined, with a smooth consistency throughout.
4. Wash the raspberries and pat them dry with paper towels. Roughly chop them on a cutting board using a chef's knife. Make sure your parents are supervising! If you are not comfortable using a knife, get your parent to do the chopping for you.
5. Zest half of a lemon with a fine zester – the smaller the holes in the zester, the finer the zest!
6. Add the chopped raspberries, as well as the zest and 5 drops of red food coloring to the cake batter. Stir well until everything is combined.
7. Spoon the batter into your lined muffin tin, about ¾ of the way full.
8. Place in preheated oven. Bake for 8 – 10 minutes (for mini cupcakes) or 18 – 22 minutes (for medium to large cupcakes).
9. Leave the cupcakes in the muffin tin until they are cool enough to touch. Then transfer them to paper towels or a tea towel to cool completely.
10. Prepare the Basic Vanilla Frosting recipe found on page 267 and add 3 – 5 drops of yellow food coloring. Beat well.
11. Load the frosting into a piping bag with a large star tip. Pipe star shaped dollops onto the cupcakes by simply pressing icing out of the bag and pulling up once a star shape has formed. Do this all over the top of each cupcakes so that each one is completely covered in stars.
12. Bend each of the bendy straws and cut them 1.5 inches below the bend. Stick one straw into the top of each cupcake, off to one side to look like a straw resting in a glass of lemonade.

Makes 18 – 20 large cupcakes or 40+ mini cupcakes (good for larger groups)

Spooky Spider Webs

Pumpkin spice is all the rage come fall, so I thought it would be great to create a delicious pumpkin cupcake recipe. The look is completed with a spider web of melted chocolate or add some extra sweetness that kids and adults will enjoy.

Allergy Information
This recipe does not call for any dairy, nuts, peanuts, or citrus.

Tools You Will Need
A large mixing bowl
Measuring cups and spoons
A fork or whisk
A spoon
Muffin tin and paper liners
A small mixing bowl
A double boiler or a microwave
Zip-top plastic sandwich bag

Ingredients
½ cup vegetable oil
3 large eggs
2 tsp pure vanilla extract
¾ cup of water
1 cup all purpose flour
A pinch of salt
1 tsp baking soda
2 tsp baking powder
¾ cup sugar
1 tsp ground cinnamon
1 tsp ground ginger

½ cup chocolate chips
¾ cup confectioner's sugar
2 tsp water

Method

1. Preheat your oven to 375F and line your muffin tin with paper liners.

2. In a large bowl combine the eggs, water, oil, pumpkin puree, and pure vanilla extract. Beat very well, until it is very smooth.

3. Add the sugar, flour, cinnamon, ginger, salt, baking soda, and baking powder all at once. Start slowly folding the batter, then beat it faster to combine all the ingredients. Beat well, for about 1 minute, until the batter is very smooth and creamy.

4. Spoon the batter into the lined muffin cups. When they are all filled, place in your preheated oven and bake for 22 – 24 minutes (for large cupcakes) or 10 – 12 minutes for mini cupcakes. The tops will be slightly golden and a toothpick inserted in the center will come out clean.

5. Leave the cupcakes in the pan until they are cool enough to touch, then transfer them to a tea towel or paper towels to cool completely.

6. In a small bowl combine the confectioner's sugar and water. Mix well until it forms a thick paste. This is your glaze for the cupcakes. When the cupcakes are fully cooled, dip the tops in the glaze (or use a spoon to pour over) and then set them to the side to dry. You can speed up the drying by putting them in the fridge.

7. Melt your chocolate chips either in a double boiler or in the microwave. Have your parents help with this, as hot melted chocolate can burn you! If you use a double boiler, stir constantly until it is fully melted. If you are microwaving the chocolate, about 1 minute should be enough, but the time will vary depending on your microwave. When you remove them from the microwave use an oven mitt, and then stir very well with a dry spoon until they are creamy. Transfer the melted chocolate to a zip-top sandwich bag. Use scissors to snip off a small corner. Then use the bag like a pastry bag to do a spider web design.

   To do a spider web design, first draw lines across the cupcake that intersect at the middle – like the spokes of a wheel. Then draw circles that cross through the lines, connecting them. You can also draw a little spider by making a small circle for the body and then 8 lines coming out from it (4 on each side) for the legs.

Makes 12 large cupcakes or 35 – 40 mini cupcakes

Princess Pear Mini Cakes

I have to admit that the name for this recipe was derived from my favourite video game character: Princess Peach. They have a light and mild flavor, thick texture – similar to a pound cake – and are presented like a layer cake. Perfect for any petit (video gaming) princess!

Allergy Information
This recipe does not call for any dairy, nuts, peanuts, or citrus.

Tools You Will Need
Measuring cups and spoons
A medium mixing bowl
Cutting board and knife
Vegetable peeler
Medium saucepan
A fork and a spoon

Ingredients
3 Bosque pears
1 tbsp white sugar
2 ½ cups of water
1 tsp ground cinnamon
2 ½ cups of all purpose flour
1 ½ tsp of baking powder
½ tsp baking soda
pinch of salt
½ cup of rice milk (or you can use coconut milk, fruit juice, flax milk, oat milk, hemp milk, water, etc.)
¾ cup of vegan butter or shortening
1 cup of sugar
1 tsp of honey
1 tsp of vanilla
3 large eggs

Method
1. Preheat your oven to 375F and line a muffin tin with paper cupcake liners.
2. Peel and core 2 Bosque pears and cut them into quarters. (If you are in a rush, you can use a pear-flavored apple-sauce and skip steps 2 – 4.) Peeling can be tricky, so make sure you have a parent helping or guiding you through it.

3. Place the pear quarters in a pot with about 2.5 cups of water (just enough to cover the pears) and a tbsp of sugar. Simmer until the pears are softened, about ten minutes.

4. Remove the softened pears from the water and mash them with a fork (you can also blend them with a hand blender if you prefer a smoother texture). Set aside to cool.

5. To make the cake, first cream vegan butter or shortening with honey and sugar until the mixture is fluffy. You can do this with a regular dinner fork, using mashing motions to smooth it out.

6. Add the vanilla and eggs, and beat it well with a fork.

7. In a separate bowl mix the flour, baking soda, baking powder, and salt.

8. Add rice milk and the flour mixture alternately (half of either at a time) to the bowl of wet ingredients (eggs, vegan butter, sugar and honey) and beat it well with a fork, but do not over beat it.

9. Then add the mashed pear and a tsp of cinnamon, and blend with a fork until it is well combined.

10. Spoon the batter into your lined muffin tin and place in a preheated 375F oven. Bake for 20 – 25 minutes, until golden brown on top and toothpick inserted in the middle comes out clean.

11. Leave the cupcakes in the muffin tin until they are cool enough to touch. Then transfer them to paper towels or a tea towel to cool completely.

12. To create mini layer cakes, first prepare the basic frosting recipe found on page 267 and add 4 drops of red food coloring to make a deep pink shade. You can do this while the cupcakes are cooling to save time.

13. Then, carefully peel the paper liners off each cupcake. Lay the cupcake on its side and slice it into two or three layers – it's up to you! Do this for each cupcake, but make sure you keep them stacked together so you don't get the layers mixed up between different cupcakes. You want them to line up in a proper stack in the end.

14. Ice a thick layer of frosting on the bottom layer of the first cupcake. Then place the second layer of cake on top. Ice a thick layer of frosting on top of that layer. Then place the top on. You can ice the top layer as well, and add whatever sprinkles or designs you prefer. Icing the sides will give the mini cakes more of a polished, chic look, while not icing them will make them look more rustic and cute.

Makes 12 large cupcakes or 35 – 40 mini cupcakes

Ultimate Rockin' Chocolate!

Dense, moist cupcakes for the cocoa crazed!

Allergy Information
This recipe does not call for any dairy, nuts, peanuts, or citrus.

Tools You Will Need
A fork or whisk
Medium mixing bowl
Measuring cups and spoons
A spoon
Muffin pan and paper liners

Ingredients
²/₃ cup vegetable oil
¾ cup water (or rice milk, or juice)

2 large eggs
1 tsp pure vanilla extract
1 cup all purpose flour
½ cup sugar
1 tsp baking soda
1 ½ tsp baking powder
A pinch of salt
½ cup cocoa
¹/₃ cup dairy-free chocolate chips (available in health food stores)

Method
1. Preheat oven to 375F and line muffin pan with paper muffin cups.
2. In a medium mixing bowl, combine the eggs, oil, water, and vanilla. Beat well with a fork.
3. Add the sugar and beat well again, until everything is combined.
4. Add the flour, baking powder, baking soda, salt, and cocoa to the wet ingredients. Stir it all up until it is well combined, about 2 minutes worth of constant stirring.
5. If you choose to add chocolate chips, add them now. Fold them in with your fork, but do not over mix the batter.
6. Spoon the batter into your lined muffin cups and place in the preheated 375F oven. Bake for 18 minutes (for medium to large cupcakes) or 8 – 10 minutes (for mini cupcakes).
7. Leave them in the muffin pan until they are cool enough to touch. Then transfer them to a tea towel or paper towels to cool completely.
8. Prepare the Basic Frosting recipe found on page 267, but substitute ¹/₃ cup of confectioner's sugar with cocoa if you want the frosting to be chocolate as well. Chocolate frosting will be a little firmer than plain vanilla frosting. Then ice the cupcakes to your liking using either a pastry bag or a butter knife or spatula.

* You can add ½ tsp of ground cinnamon to the frosting for an extra blast of flavor!

Makes 12 large cupcakes, or 16 – 18 medium cupcakes, or 30 – 38 mini cupcakes

Warm Spice Cupcakes

Almost more muffin than cupcake, these delicious morsels are decorated to look like little apples which makes them fit thematically for the fall or back to school. They are flavored with the rich spiciness of cinnamon and the warmth of apple. This particular recipe has proven to be a fan favorite amongst my friends and colleagues, as I discovered after bringing a tray of them in to work.

Allergy information
This recipe does not call for any dairy, nuts, peanuts, or citrus.

Tools You Will Need
Medium mixing bowl
A fork or electric mixer
A spoon
Measuring cups and spoons

Ingredients
½ cup vegan margarine or shortening
1 cup sugar
1 tsp vanilla
2 eggs
¾ cup water
1 tsp baking soda
1 ½ tsp baking powder
1 ½ cups flour
A dash of salt
1 tsp cinnamon
1 ½ tsp ground cloves
¾ tsp cardamom
¼ cup brown sugar
½ cup unsweetened applesauce

Topping
One straight pretzel and one leaf of oregano or mint for each cupcake

Method

1. Preheat oven to 375F and line muffin tin with paper liners.

2. Cream together the vegan margarine or shortening with the white sugar using a fork. To cream them together means to smooth them out and combine them well at the same time. You can use an electric mixer to do this to make it easier and faster.

3. Add the eggs and vanilla and mix well.

4. Add the water and mix well. It will appear almost curdled, but that is normal.

5. Add half of the flour and mix until just combined. Then add the rest of the flour, the baking powder, baking soda, salt, cardamom, cinnamon, and cloves all at once. Mix until everything is well combined.

6. Then fold in the applesauce and the brown sugar using a spoon, until the batter looks streaky. It should not be fully combined, and do not over mix.

7. Spoon the batter into your lined muffin tin and place in the preheated oven. Bake for 18 – 22 minutes (for medium to large cupcakes) or 8 – 10 minutes (for mini cupcakes). The cupcakes are done when a toothpick inserted in the center comes out clean. The tops will not rise very much, they will stay almost flat.

8. To make them look like little apples, first prepare a batch of the Basic Frosting recipe found on page 267 and add either 8 drops of green food coloring to make them look like Granny Smith apples, or 10 drops of red food coloring to look like a McIntosh apple.

9. You can either frost the cupcakes with a butter knife, or you can use a piping bag to create a basic swirl design. Then simply pop one pretzel into the center of each cupcake and tuck a leaf of oregano next to the pretzel. Fresh oregano is readily available at grocery stores, but if you don't have any you can create the same look by adding more green food coloring to a small portion of the icing. Then use a pastry bag with a thin tip to draw on a leaf design.

Makes 12 large cupcakes, or 16 – 18 medium cupcakes, or 30 – 38 mini cupcakes

MASH-UPS

Once you've become confident at making a particular recipe it's a great idea to mash it together with another dessert item to make a new "mash-up." Brownies and cookies baked together, or cookie dough baked into a little bowl filled with sorbet, they're all great ways to combine your favorite recipes into one mega recipe for something new and fun. I've provided a few of my personal favorites as suggestions, but why not try out your own mash-ups at home!

Brownie Trifle

Allergen Information

This recipe does not call for any dairy, nuts, or peanuts.
This recipe can be made egg-free by using the egg-free brownie recipe.

Tools You Will Need

Large metal mixing bowl
Small saucepan
Whisk
Measuring cups and spoons
Several small glasses, mugs, or bowls for serving
Fork
Small bowl

Ingredients

1 batch of any brownie recipe from this book
1 cup Enjoy Life chocolate mega chunks
1 tbsp Rice Dream or Coconut Dream
½ tsp pure vanilla extract
½ tsp ground cinnamon (optional)
1 tsp malt powder (optional)
½ cup mashed raspberries
1 cup whole raspberries

Method

1. Prepare 1 batch of any type of brownies from this book (gluten-free, fudgy, or egg-free) and then set aside to come to room temperature.
2. To make the chocolate filling, fill a small saucepan with water about 1 inch deep. Place a medium-sized metal mixing bowl on top and turn the heat to medium low to create a double boiler. Add the chocolate, vanilla, and Rice Dream to the bowl and begin to slowly stir using a whisk until all the chocolate has melted. Take the bowl off the saucepan and remove from the heat. If you want to flavor it with malt powder and cinnamon, add them now and whisk well.

3. To assemble the trifle, first cut sections of brownie to fit your serving glass. Each serving glass should have 2 layers of brownie, one on the bottom and one in the middle. Line the bottom of each glass with brownie.

4. Drizzle a little bit of the chocolate filling onto the brownie.

5. Mash ½ cup of raspberries in a small bowl using a fork. Add a scoop of mashed raspberry to each serving glass on top of the filling.

6. Add another drizzle of chocolate filling if you desire. Then layer another piece of brownie on top. Finish it off with a little bit more chocolate filling and then some whole raspberries.

Makes 4 – 6 servings

Cookie-Bottom Cupcakes

Allergen Information

Refer to allergen information attached to each cookie and cake recipe used.

Ingredients

1 batch of Ultimate Rockin' Chocolate cupcakes, Chocolate Cinnamon muffins, or basic egg-free cupcakes
½ batch of chocolate chip cookie dough, fudgy sandwich cookie dough (less the filling), or shaped sugar cookie dough

Method

1. Preheat oven to 375F and line a muffin pan with paper muffin liners.
2. Prepare half a batch of any of the cookie doughs listed above and refrigerate until ready to use.
3. Prepare a batch of any of the cupcake batters listed above and set aside. Play around with the combinations of cookie dough and cake batter to see what unique flavor combinations you can come up with!
4. Pull off chunks of dough about the size of a US coin and roll into a ball with your hand. Place them in the lined muffin cups and gently squish down with your thumb to flatten.
5. Pour cake batter on top of the cookie dough, filling the muffin cups about ¾ full.
6. Place the muffin tray in preheated oven and bake according to the time indicated in the cake recipe.

Makes 16 – 18 servings

Chocolate Chip Cookie Brownie

Allergen Information

This recipe does not call for any dairy, nuts, or peanuts.

Ingredients

½ batch of chocolate chip cookie dough (page 89)
1 batch of fudgy brownies (page 121) or gluten-free brownies

Method

1. Preheat oven to 350F.
2. Prepare half a batch of chocolate chip cookies.
3. Line a square or round 8 inch cake pan with parchment paper. Press the cookie dough into the bottom of the pan making sure the layer is an even thickness. Refrigerate for 30 minutes to allow the dough to firm up.
4. Prepare 1 batch of fudgy brownies and pour the finished batter directly on top of the cooled cookie dough. Smooth out with a spoon.
5. Place the pan in preheated oven and bake for 35 – 40 minutes, until a toothpick inserted into the brownie comes out clean. The brownie batter will still be a bit soft once it's finished baking but will become firm if refrigerated.
6. When cooled, cut into 1 inch squares using a smooth knife. To make the cutting easier, run the knife through hot water and lightly dry off with a cloth first.

Makes 15 – 20 squares

Cookie Bowl with Sorbet

Allergen Information

Refer to allergen information attached to each cookie and cake recipe used.

Ingredients

Double batch of any sorbet/ice cream listed in this book (or 1 batch of fruit punch sorbet)
1 batch of any cookie dough from this book

Method

1. Prepare the cookie bowls ahead of time to allow them adequate cooling time. They should be completely chilled when you use them. The best doughs for this recipe include chocolate chip cookie dough, fudgy sandwich cookie dough, maple molasses cookie dough, sprinkle fun cookie dough, and salted honey and mint cookie dough.
2. Preheat oven to 375F and line a muffin pan with paper muffin liners.
3. Press enough cookie dough into each muffin cup to line the bottom and sides. It should be about inches thickness all around.
4. Place in preheated oven and bake for 9 – 12 minutes, until the bowls have browned on the edges. If the dough is too soft it won't hold its shape when you remove the paper liners. Remove the pan from the oven halfway through baking and use a spoon to press down the middle.
5. Once they're finished baking, remove from the oven and allow to cool fully while you prepare the sorbet or ice cream. You may need to press the center in with a spoon again before they cool.
6. When the sorbet/ice cream is ready, peel the paper liners off the cookie bowls and scoop in the frozen dessert.
7. Serve immediately.

Makes 12 – 15 servings

EXTRA BITES AND BASICS

This chapter contains simple basics and some no-bake recipes that call for minimal ingredients and can be used in place of store-bought brands. You'll find strawberry jam and applesauce that are better than name brands and coconut cream drizzle that can replace dairy-based creams as a sauce. Granola, fritters, and rice pudding are just some more examples of the extra bites you will learn how to make in this chapter.

Coconut Sunbutter Balls

With only 5 ingredients and no oven required, this is a great recipe for those on the go! And it packs a punch of rich flavor and protein.

Allergen Information

This recipe does not call for any dairy, nuts, peanuts, citrus, egg, or gluten.

What you will need

Measuring cup
Mixing bowl
Spoon
Tray or baking sheet lined with parchment paper

Ingredients

¼ cup Sunbutter sunflower seed spread (chunky or smooth)
1 cup shredded coconut flakes (Let's Do Organic brand)
¼ cup maple syrup
5 tbsp brown sugar
A pinch of salt

Method

1. Line a tray or baking sheet with parchment paper to prevent the dessert from sticking.
2. Add the ingredients all at once to a mixing bowl and stir until everything is well combined and there are no lumps of brown sugar remaining. It should come together in a dough-like clump.
3. Spoon out small portions of the dough about the size of a US coin. Roll them into a ball using your palms and set them on the tray, making sure that they are spaced apart.
4. You can roll them in extra coconut flakes or chocolate shavings to your liking, or just leave them plain.
5. Refrigerate for a minimum of 1 hour until they have firmed up.

Makes 25 pieces

Coconut Cream Drizzle

An excellent substitute for dairy-based creams, this can be used for dipping scones, drizzling on crepes, cakes, and any type of pastry for a boost of extra flavor. It will last for up to 4 days in the fridge if stored in an air-tight container.

Allergen Information

This recipe does not call for any dairy, nuts, peanuts, citrus, or egg.

Tools You Will Need

Blender
Spoon
Mason jar with lid
Measuring cup

Ingredients

The fat from one can of coconut milk plus ¼ cup of the water
5 heaping tbsp of confectioner's sugar
Pinch of salt
½ tsp pure vanilla extract
1 tsp honey

Method

1. If you aren't familiar with coconut milk, you might be surprised by its texture when bought in a can as opposed to coconut milk meant for drinking that comes in a tetra-pak. When you open the can it will be filled with a thick layer of fat on top with about $^1/_2$ cup of coconut water on the bottom. Do not use light coconut milk for this recipe as it does not have a high enough fat content. Scoop the fat into your blender, along with $^1/_4$ cup of the water from the bottom.
2. Add the confectioner's sugar (this does not have to be measured precisely. You can just eyeball it with a regular spoon), pure vanilla extract, salt, and honey (again, the vanilla and honey can be eyeballed).
3. Blend for 1 minute, then shake to stir up clumps in the bottom. Blend again for 1 minute.
4. Pour the mixture into a mason jar for storage. It can be used right away, though it will have a thicker consistency if you refrigerate for a half hour. It will last in the fridge for up to 3 days in a sealed container.

Makes 1 pint jar

Strawberry Jam

Gooey strawberries with hints of vanilla and lime. Spread it on toast, as a layer in pound cake, a filling for tarts, or just a spoonful on its own! Homemade jam always beats the store bought varieties. It will last for up to 5 days in the fridge if stored in an air-tight container.

Allergen Information

This recipe does not call for any dairy, nuts, peanuts, egg, or gluten.

Tools You Will Need

Medium saucepan
Zester
Paring knife
Cutting board
Measuring cups and spoons
Mason jar with lid
Mixing spoon

Ingredients

2 lbs fresh strawberries
3 tbsp organic honey
1 tsp pure vanilla extract
Zest of ¼ of a lime
$^1/_3$ cup of sugar

Method

1. Remove the stems of the strawberries and cut into quarters.
2. Add them to a medium saucepan along with the honey, zest, vanilla, and sugar.
3. Turn to medium heat and stir well.
4. When it starts bubbling, turn to low and let simmer for 1 hour, stirring often to prevent sticking or burning.
5. After an hour turn the heat off and let the jam cool for 20 minutes. Then pour it into a mason jar and let cool completely before covering with a lid and refrigerating. If using on pancakes, waffles, or scones, you may want to serve it while still hot.

Makes 1 pint jar of jam

Granola

Allergen-free granola is pretty hard to find, and personally I prefer the kind I make at home to the ones I have been able to find in the store. The great thing about granola is that you can easily change the ingredients to suit what you have in your cupboards. For example, you can add slices of dried apricots or other dried fruits, you can leave out the raisins, or you can use quinoa instant "oats" instead of oats from wheat. Granola is a great breakfast or snack food and is a great little extra to tuck away in a lunch box.

Allergen Information

This recipe does not call for any dairy, nuts, citrus, or peanuts.

Tools You Will Need

Medium mixing bowl
Spatula
Measuring cups and spoons
Baking sheet
Parchment paper

Ingredients

1 egg white
1 tbsp vegetable oil

1 tsp ground ginger
½ tsp ground cinnamon
¼ tsp ground cardamom
½ cup oats (can be substituted with quinoa instant "oats")
Handful of raisins
⅓ cup dried coconut flakes
2 tbsp brown sugar
1 tbsp maple syrup (can be substituted with honey)
Pinch of salt
2 tbsp Enjoy Life mini chocolate chips (optional)

Method

The measurements for this recipe are very loose and can be altered to suit your tastes without hesitation. The egg can easily be swapped out for ¼ cup honey or maple syrup.

1. Preheat oven to 400F and line a baking sheet with parchment paper.
2. Add all ingredients except the egg and oil to a medium mixing bowl and fold together using a spatula.
3. Add the egg white and oil and mix well.
4. Pour the mixture onto the lined baking sheet and spread it around evenly. Try not to break up any clumps as they add a nice texture to the granola.
5. Place the baking sheet in preheated oven and bake for 8 minutes.
6. Allow to cool completely before scooping into a bowl or mason jar to serve. This goes really well with fresh seasonal fruit.

Crunchy 'n Smooth Marshmallow Cupcakes

Cake is wonderful, but sometimes you crave a change of taste. Swap the cake out altogether and make Rice Krispies cupcakes that are so simple yet so satisfying. This dessert is definitely for the kid with a major sweet tooth!

Allergy Information

This recipe does not call for any dairy, nuts, peanuts, citrus, or egg.

This recipe can be made gluten-free by substituting Rice Krispies cereal for brown rice gluten-free Rice Krispies, and by using gluten-free marshmallows which are generally available in major grocery stores.

What You Will Need

A large pot
Wooden spoon
Muffin tin
Paper towel
Pastry bag with round piping tip

Ingredients

1 tbsp vegetable oil
225 – 250g marshmallows
250g Rice Krispies (preferably gluten-free)
Basic Frosting Recipe (see page 267)
Extra vegetable oil for greasing the pan

Method

1. Dab some vegetable oil on a paper towel or napkin and run it along the inside and bottom of the muffin tin. Do not over grease, a light coating is enough.
2. Warm the vegetable oil in a large pot on medium heat.
3. Add the marshmallows and start stirring constantly with a wooden spoon, scraping the bottom often to make sure they don't burn. Small marshmallows work better for this because they melt much faster.
4. Once the marshmallows are melted, turn off the heat and move them to a cool burner. Then get an extra pair of hands to pour the puffed rice cereal into the pot while you keep on stirring. Try to mix the ingredients in evenly by breaking up large pockets of marshmallow or cereal. The cereal should be completely coated in marshmallow.
5. As soon as the mixture is well combined, wet your fingertips with water. Spoon a scoop of the mixture into each of the cups in the muffin tin and press each one into place firmly, so that it takes the shape of the cup. It should be cool enough to touch by this point, as it cools quickly after removing it from the heat. You do not need muffin cups or liners for this recipe.
6. Remove the Marshmallow Dream cupcakes from the muffin tin and set them on a separate plate.
7. Prepare the Basic Frosting recipe found on page 267. If you are in a hurry, you can use smooth marshmallow from a jar, which is found in most grocery stores. Just be sure to read the ingredients to make sure it does not contain any of the allergens you are trying to avoid.
8. Load the topping into your pastry bag and do any kind of swirl design you like!

Makes 16 large cupcakes or 32 mini cupcakes

Fritti

Allergen Information

This recipe does not call for any dairy, nuts, citrus, or peanuts.

Tools You Will Need	Ingredients
Manual pasta maker or pasta attachment for your electric mixer	2 large eggs
	2 tbsp sugar
Large bowl	2 tbsp olive oil
Whisk	2 tbsp water
Measuring cups and spoons	2 cups flour
Large pot	¼ cup confectioner's sugar
Oven mitts	
Slotted spoon or spider	1 L vegetable oil
Knife	
Large pan or platter for serving	*It is traditional to use white wine instead of water in
10 paper towels	this recipe

Method

1. Combine the water and sugar in a large bowl and make a well in the center.
2. Pour the eggs, water, and olive oil into the center of the well. Use a whisk to break up the eggs.
3. You can either use your clean fingers or a whisk to slowly start incorporating the flour into the center of the well. It will form thick dough.
4. Dust the dough with some flour to prevent sticking. Begin passing the first half of the dough through the pasta maker starting on the widest setting to flatten and stretch it out. Each time you pass it through the rollers, move the dial to the next thickness until you reach the thinnest setting.
5. Use a knife or scalloped edge pasta cutter to slice the dough into sections about 1 inch wide by 4 inches long. You don't have to be at all precise with this.
6. Line a baking tray or platter with paper towels and set aside.
7. Heat 1 L of vegetable oil in a large pot until it starts to simmer but not boil. Drop a scrap of dough into the oil to test the temperature. It should start bubbling and frying (but not burning) right away. If it sinks to the bottom and doesn't bubble, the oil is not yet hot enough. If it starts boiling hard or burning, the oil is too hot and you need to reduce the heat and wait for it to reach the right temperature.
8. Drop the strips of dough into the oil (always drop items into hot oil away from your body) one at a time, so there are about 4 or 5 frying at a time depending on the size of your pot. They only take 15 – 20 seconds on each side. You can use a slotted spoon or a spider to flip them over. They are finished frying when they are golden brown on both sides. Use a slotted spoon or spider to remove them from the oil and drop them onto the lined tray or platter.
9. Repeat until each strip of dough has been fried.
10. Dust with confectioner's sugar to your liking.

Makes about 25 – 30 medium – sized fritti

Rice Pudding

Rice pudding is one of those things that I have always wanted to order for dessert in a restaurant, but have never been able to find dairy-free. So I developed my own recipe using coconut and rice milks, as well as the natural creaminess of Arborio rice to stand in for the texture of dairy.

Allergen Information

This recipe does not call for any dairy, nuts, peanuts, egg, or gluten.

Tools You Will Need

Medium saucepan
Measuring cups and spoons
4 small serving bowls
Spatula or wooden spoon
Paring knife
Zester

Ingredients

1 naval orange
¾ cup short grain Arborio rice
1 cup Rice Dream
1 cup Coconut Dream
1 tsp pure vanilla extract
1 tbsp organic honey
2 tbsp confectioner's sugar
Pinch of salt
1 tsp ground cinnamon
5 tbsp Earth Balance

Method

1. Add the juice and 1 tsp of the zest of 1 naval orange to a medium saucepan, along with the rice, Rice Dream, vanilla, honey, confectioner's sugar, salt, cinnamon, and Earth Balance.
2. Turn to medium-high heat and begin to stir with a wooden spoon or spatula until well combined.
3. Allow the rice to come to a boil and then reduce to medium-low heat and allow to simmer for 20 minutes, stirring well every 5 minutes to prevent it from burning on the bottom. The rice will develop a creamy color and silky texture while it's simmering away.
4. When the rice is ready, spoon it into cute serving glasses or small bowls and serve immediately. You can garnish with fresh fruit, mint leaves, cinnamon sticks and orange zest, or Enjoy Life mini chocolate chips. Or you can simply eat it as is.

Serves 5 – 6

Quick Basic Fritters

This recipe does not call for any dairy, nuts, peanuts, citrus, or egg.

Tools You Will Need

Medium pot
Slotted spoon
Large mixing bowl
Measuring cups and spoons
Whisk
Ladle
Baking sheet or large plate
Several sheets of paper towel

Ingredients

1 ½ cups all purpose flour
2 ½ tsp baking powder
A generous pinch of salt
1 tbsp sugar
½ tsp pure vanilla extract
2 cups cold ginger ale or near beer (about 1 can)
¼ cup cold water

1 L vegetable oil

Flavored sugar:

1 tsp ground cinnamon
½ tsp ground ginger
3 tbsp sugar
Pinch of salt

Method

1. In a large mixing bowl combine the flour, baking powder, salt, and sugar using a whisk.

2. Make a well in the center using either your fingers or a spoon, and pour in the water, ginger ale, and pure vanilla extract all at once. Whisk it together really well, making sure to beat out any lumps. Set the batter aside while you prepare the oil for frying. You'll notice that bubbles will start to form on the top of the batter, which give the fritters a light and fluffy texture when they're fried. If you don't have ginger ale available to you, you can also use near bear (alcohol-free beer) which gives the fritters a malty freshly baked bread scent and can also be served with savory foods.

3. Pour the oil into the pot and turn the heat to medium. Allow the oil to heat up for about 8 minutes, making sure to keep an eye on it the whole time. Oil can overheat and burn very quickly, which can cause smoke. Test the temperature by using a spoon to drop some of the batter into the oil. If it begins to sizzle immediately and easily rises to the surface when you tap at it with a slotted spoon then it's ready for frying. If the batter sinks to the bottom and only a few bubbles form then it's still too cold. If the batter begins to brown and burn quickly then it's too hot and you need to reduce the temperature and scoop the test drop out.

4. When the oil has reached the appropriate temperature you can begin scooping the batter in, about 1 – 2 tbsp at a time to form a nice-sized fritter. Always scoop the batter into the oil in the direction away from your body, and never drop it in from a high distance. Make sure it's touching the oil and then slide it in away from you to avoid getting hit with any splashing oil. Only fry about 2 or 3 at a time or the oil will reduce in temperature. They take about one minute on each side. Use a slotted spoon to gently flip them over. When they are finished frying, scoop them out of the pot and onto a baking sheet or plate lined with paper towels to soak up excess oil. Always use a slotted spoon to avoid scooping up excess oil.

5. You can either sprinkle them with salt or sugar, or eat them plain. You can also make a really nice flavored sugar by mixing the cinnamon, ginger, sugar, and salt together in a small bowl and then sprinkle it over the fritters while they're still hot.

Makes about 25 fritters

Applesauce

Allergen Information

This recipe does not call for any dairy, nuts, peanuts, egg, citrus, or gluten.

What you will need

Medium saucepan with lid
Mixing spoon
Measuring spoons
Paring knife
Vegetable peeler
Cutting board

Ingredients

5 McIntosh apples
1 heaping tbsp sugar
1 tbsp brown sugar
½ tsp ground cinnamon

Method

1. Use a vegetable peeler to remove the skin from the apples.
2. Use a paring knife to remove the core and seeds and then cut the apples up into cubes. The size isn't all that important because they will melt down as they cook.
3. Add the cubed apples, sugars, and cinnamon to a medium saucepan.
4. Turn the heat to medium and stir the apples so that they are all well coated in sugar and spice. Let them simmer on medium for about 5 minutes, stirring every minute or so. Then reduce to low and let simmer with the lid on askew (to allow some steam out) for 20 – 25 minutes. If the apples appear to be too watery you can simmer them with the lid askew for another 5 – 10 minutes on low.
5. You can serve the applesauce chunky or you can blend it to a smooth consistency once it's cooled. This can be served hot or cold.

Throwing the Perfect Tea Party

One of the best ways to display your culinary chops is to throw a wonderful party where your kids and their friends can sample all the delicious treats you've made together. And of course, if you're a kid without an upcoming birthday or in need of a birthday party theme, a tea party is a fantastic pop-up occasion. Now if you're giving me telepathic cut-eye at this point (because either your kids won't sit still for long enough to serve tea or you're the parent of 10 boys under 10), let's first straighten out that tea parties don't have to be froo froo with a coating of pink tulle. In fact you don't even have to serve real tea at all, and a simple culinary craft can be a way to engage your kids and keep them at the table. Here are some tips for throwing a memorable tea party with your kids to enjoy with their friends.

What to serve

A high tea menu traditionally consists of small bite-sized morsels that can be eaten without a knife and fork. There's typically a selection of different baked goods and finger foods to choose from, so stick with a ratio of about 1 recipe per 1 tea party attendee. If you plan to have more than 5 or 6 kids (or kids and parents) coming, then 5 or 6 food options should suffice. I would also suggest that you make half batches because each guest is probably not going to consume a whole batch of cookies, for example.

Making 2 or 3 simple recipes really well is better than making 4 or 5 recipes moderately well. I would suggest scones, brownies, and squares of pound cake, chocolate covered fruit, or anything miniature.

Make 1 amazing showstopper (and don't be shy to present it as your showstopper)! Your guests will be wowed if you make 1 recipe that really blows their socks off, whether it's by taste or by unique and original presentation. You can spend more time on that and then fill the table with a couple other simple and quick recipes. This is a good time to try out the *Mash-ups* chapter.

Drinks can also be showstoppers. Try serving one of the hot chocolate recipes in the *Everything Chocolate* chapter, or a soda float found in the *From the Freezer* chapter.

Location & decoration

What's the weather like outside? Can you have your party outdoors? If yes, why not have it on a picnic blanket!

What will you sit on? Floor cushions on the ground, around a picnic table, or at your kids-sized table?

Add some height to your spread by using tiered serving plates. Add some color with mismatched tea cups and serving plates. And add texture with napkins, placemats, tablecloths, and flowers. Most importantly, make sure the décor is age appropriate. For little kids you will likely want to stick with unbreakable place settings.

For little tots, fill in empty seats with their favorite stuffed animals – and don't forget the name tags!

Decorate with spreads and dippables. This is where homemade jam, applesauce, or coconut cream drizzle come into play. Letting your guests spread and dip their food engages them in the party while also adding pops of color.

Activities

Keeping kids engaged can be as simple as letting them decorate their own cupcake or gingerbread cookie. Kids don't necessarily care which cupcakes are the prettiest or have the most intricate frosting. They will get joy and satisfaction out of doing it for themselves. Try putting out bowls of frosting with plastic spatulas and piping bags (filled ahead of time) so they can get creative on their own.

A great activity for middle-grade kids is decorating personal place cards made with rectangular gingerbread cookies and fine tipped piping bags.

FROSTING

Basic Frosting Recipe

A basic frosting recipe that can be easily transformed into many different flavors.

Allergen Information

This recipe does not call for any dairy, nuts, peanuts, legumes, egg, or citrus. It can also be easily made gluten-free, as there are many brands of gluten-free vegan butter and confectioner's sugar. Icing sugars that are made from pure sugar or sugar and corn starch are gluten-free. Ingredients such as **modified food starch**, for example, contain gluten. If you are unsure about an ingredient, check the Canadian Celiac Association's website.

What You Will Need

A large mixing bowl
A fork, flat spatula, or electric beater
Piping bag for decoration (See instructions below on how to use a piping bag and the parts required)

Ingredients

1 cup vegan butter or vegetable shortening or lard
1 tsp vanilla extract
4 ½ to 5 cups confectioner's sugar

Method

The measurements used to make frosting are not firm, as they can change depending on humidity, heat, and also the brands/products you are using. Some vegan butters are very solid or waxy, so you may need to loosen it up by adding a liquid (this can be juice, rice milk, or coconut milk, for example) 1 tsp at a time in between additions of confectioner's sugar. Shortening will have a very fluffy texture, while lard may be heavier. You can lighten it up by whipping it on high speed with an electric beater.

Also remember that adding food coloring will thin out the frosting, so you may need to add a few tbsp more confectioner's sugar to thicken it after adding the color. For pastel colors, more confectioner's sugar is not usually needed. It is when you are creating a bright or deep color (adding more than a tbsp of color) that it will need some thickening up.

1. Let the vegan butter soften at room temperature until it is soft enough to mash with a fork. Then add it all at once to the mixing bowl and begin to beat it on medium speed until it is creamy. If you are using a fork or spatula, it will take some elbow grease!

2. Once it is creamy and there are no lumps, add the vanilla and beat well on high speed.

3. Add the confectioner's sugar half a cup at a time so that it doesn't spray all over you. For each addition, start mixing on low speed until it starts to combine, and then speed it up to high speed to mix it well and give it a fluffy texture.

4. Save the food coloring until the very end, and then add more confectioner's sugar if needed.

5. For colors like deep red you will have to use possibly 2 tbsp of food coloring. To lessen the amount of food coloring you will need, use a food pigment that has a more gel-like texture.

How to use a piping bag

1. Select the tip you would like to use. For a swirly design, use a star tip. For a smooth design, use a round tip. And for little details or patterns, use a fine round tip.

2. Take a plastic piping bag and snip the tip off with a pair of scissors. One inch should be snipped off for a large tip, while only 3/4 of an inch should be snipped off for a fine tip.

3. If you are using a large tip, simply slide it into the piping bag and push it through the hole you cut until it is snugly in place. Then scoop your frosting into the bag, leaving at least 2 inches of room at the top. Twist the top of the bag tightly to close it and prevent the frosting from seeping out. When icing your cupcakes, squeeze the frosting out by putting pressure at the top of the bag – not the middle or near the tip. This will ensure your frosting does not seep out the top of the bag.

4. For fine piping tips, you will need a plastic attachment called a "coupler."

5. Press the coupler down into the hole you created in the tip of the piping bag so that it is firmly in place but sticking out the end. Then place your tip over the coupler. Take the coupler ring and screw it into place over the tip and the first part of the coupler. This will ensure that your tip stays in place while icing your cupcakes. Scoop your frosting into the piping bag, leaving 2 inches free at the top. Twist the top until it is firmly closed, and squeeze from the top of the bag to push the frosting through the tip.

GET CREATIVE!

Get inspired and be creative!

The best cupcake recipes call for love and creativity, so brainstorm your own ideas and try them out. A recipe is just a jumping point to get your creative juices flowing, so you should always try to add a bit of your own flare.

How you decorate your cupcakes is entirely up to you. This book provides some suggestions, but you are free to follow your own lead and present them however you like. Presentation is a very important part of the baking process, because it can create a mood (funky, chic, cute), describe the cake flavor, and get your friends oohing and aahhing over your artistic skills!

Take a minute to think about what inspires you, and what displays your personality . . .

Ingredients and flavors

What do you have in your cupboards? Cereals, marshmallows of different colors and sizes, jams, pretzels, dried fruits, coconut flakes, and other dry ingredients can jazz up a cupcake or bedazzle any frosting. Try smashing up some graham crackers and brown sugar to make a topping that looks like sand for a tropical party.

Do you have any leftover holiday snacks like cinnamon hearts, candy canes, or candy corn lying around? These can be chopped up, stacked on top of icing, or broken into pieces – play with texture!

Open up the fridge. What kinds of berries, citrus, tropical, or basic fruits do you see? A bit of citrus zest can give some zing to your frosting or cake batter – or both!

What do you see in the spice cabinet? Cinnamon, cloves, ginger, cardamom and allspice are warm, savory flavors. Essences such as vanilla and mint will add a mellow flavor. Honey or maple syrup are great natural sweeteners that can also be used as a decorative drizzle. Try combining different spices and sweeteners with whatever fruits you have available.

Juice is a joy to work with, because it can add loads of flavor with little effort. Just replace water for the same measurement of your favorite fruit juice. Pineapple cupcakes anyone?

Maybe you have some sprinkles or shimmer powder left over from birthdays past. You can always use them if you're in a pinch, but you can modify them slightly by contrasting or coordinating colors, sprinkling them only on half the cupcake or in stripes, loading the frosting with tons of sprinkles or just giving them a light dusting of shimmer. The level of intensity is up to you.

Presentation

You eat with your eyes first so make sure your cupcakes are dressed to impress.

Cupcakes aren't bound to their wrappers. Peel the wrappers off and use basic shaped cookie cutters to make them different shapes and sizes. Or you can buy pans that are already shaped. Mini doughnuts and mini loaf pans are easy to find in your local home store. Make heart shaped cupcakes for Valentines Day!

You can also use wrappers that have funky prints and colors, or shaped edges to add some pizzazz. A lacy edged wrapper will be chic enough for any tea party or closet fashion show.

Frosting

The number of ways you can use basic frosting are endless, so you should never feel stumped when icing your cakes. When in doubt, you can always use different shapes and sizes of piping tips to do a basic swirl on your cupcakes. It is a good idea to have a variety of piping tips in your cupboard so that you can do more detailed designs.

Inspiration is everywhere you look! Below is a list of possibilities – take these ideas and make them your own. Whether you decide to keep it simple or crazy intricate, your cupcakes will always look unique and delicious. Remember that your skills improve with practice. If you were a little rusty this time around at making that perfect swirl or piping the planet earth–it's no big deal. Your friends will be gobbling them up faster than you can frost 'em!

Artistic Possibilities

Look up at the sky. Is it full of fluffy white clouds, a bright sun, or plump raindrops? Mid-size round piping tips can help you create a fluffy effect.

What season is it? Autumn is full of leaves, spring brings flowers, snowflakes fall in winter, and summer feels like a day at the beach. Get inspired by your natural surroundings, after all, you are using natural ingredients.

Is there a robin perched in your tree? Or maybe an owl? Make your cupcakes quirky and cute by making cartoon versions of their faces with exaggerated eyes and beaks!

What is your favorite animal print? Leopards and zebras have some sassy skins.

Pretty flowers can be any color palette or size. They can be neon and groovy, or petite and pastel.

Why not make a silhouette of a tree by piping it on with black icing? Or use a small star tip to make leaves for a realistic looking tree?

Are you bursting with personality? Ice your cupcakes with bright yellow and then use black frosting with a thin piping tip to make emoticon faces!
Mini cupcakes can be made to look like a sea of eyeballs for a Halloween themed party.

Personalize your cupcakes by drawing the letter of your first name on each one. Use any style writing you can dream of, from chunky block letters to delicate cursive. You can perk it up with a bit of shimmer powder!

For the astronomy buffs out there, try making each cupcake look like a different planet or star, then present them all together to form our universe.

If school's out for winter or summer vacation, create a simple palm tree or a beach ball. Let your class know you've got the travel bug!

Every princess needs her bling, so give your cupcakes some real flavor with cake sparkles, sugar decorating pearls, and mini crowns.

Don't forget about your puppy! Celebrate your pooch's birthday in style with paw print adorned cupcakes. Spice them up by layering a bright frosting color as a base, with a piped-on paw print in white.

Hit your designs out of the park by turning cupcakes into baseballs, basketballs, or whatever sport you live for. Frost a cupcake with a base color the same color as the ball, then load the stitching colored icing into a piping bag with a thin round tip. Make little dashes in an arc shape on either side to create the effect of a sports ball.

Patterns and shapes are simple and fun. If you're new to cake decorating, it is a good place to start. Adorn your cupcakes with polka dots, stripes, swirls, and geometric shapes. Use contrasting colors for the base layer of icing and the patterns or shapes to make it pop!

Allergy Indicator Sheet

It is handy have a sheet outlining what your (or your child's) allergies are to give to parents, teachers, day care supervisors, and camp counsellors. Have a few of these printed up and at the ready to hand out on first days of school, to school secretaries, family members, and anyone who may be responsible for caring for your child. A good opportunity to hand it out is when you are discussing with your child's teacher what they are allergic to and the severity of their allergies. Fill the sheet out together instead of giving your child copies to hand out without explaining what it is. It is best practice to become comfortable communicating with others about food allergies from a young age, so that your kids are confident in their approach when you are absent, or later in life when it is solely their responsibility.

Here is a sample chart using some of the most common food allergens as examples. You will have to tailor this to your child's specific needs. The list is not exhaustive, so add additional information to the categories where you see fit.

I am allergic to	This is sometimes also called	Common foods to avoid	Is this an anaphylactic allergy that requires the carrying of an Epi Pen?
Dairy	Casien, whey powder, whey protein, lactose, lactic acid, modified milk ingredients, small capital letter D or word 'dairy' printed on the bottom right hand corner of food packaging	Butter, milk, cream, yogurt, cheese, commercial baked goods (such as cookies, crackers, cakes, muffins) and frozen meals, pastries (such as puff pastry), ice cream, commercial chocolates and candies, commercial chocolate bars, frozen yogurt, commercial pre-made pizzas and burritos, cheese curd and poutine, commercial gravies and sauces	YES/NO
Nuts	Tree nuts (including all kinds of tree nuts: almonds, pistachios, pine nuts, chestnuts, Brazil, cashew, macadamia, pecan, walnut, etc.)	Nut butters, commercial baked goods, almond flour (contained in many gluten-free foods), chocolate bars, most commercial chocolates and candies, bottled sauces or marinades, trail mixes and granola bars, cereals, dried fruits and seeds	YES/NO

Peanuts	Peanut butter, peanut oil	Commercial baked goods and bottled sauces, peanut oil, peanut butter, commercial chocolate bars and candies, trail mixes and granola bars, cereals, dried fruits and seeds	YES/NO
Egg	Albumen, meringue, egg substitute, non-soy lecithins, yolk, egg white, egg wash, dried egg or egg solids	Caesar dressing, mayonnaise, egg beaters, commercial baked goods, egg breads, egg noodles/pastas, eggnog, pastries	YES/NO
Soy	Tofu, soy bean oil, soy lecithin, edamame, miso, bean sprouts, soya, soybean, tamari	Miso soup, tofu, edamame, most commercial packaged foods including baked goods, sauces, soy sauce, dressings, meats, spreads, and noodles, vegetable oils, chicken/beef/vegetable broths	YES/NO

On the next page is a blank sheet that you can reproduce and suit to your own child's allergy specifications.

I am allergic to	This is sometimes also called	Common foods to avoid	Is this an anaphylactic allergy that requires the carrying of an Epi Pen?

Substitutes

Below is a list of some substitutes for the most common food allergies.

1 large egg can be substituted with:

- $^1/_3$ cup of applesauce
- ¼ – $^1/_3$ cup of water, one tsp white vinegar, and ¼ tsp baking soda
- ¼ – $^1/_3$ cup of water, one tsp lemon juice, and ¼ tsp baking soda
- 2 tbsp sunflower seed butter

Milk in baked goods can be replaced with:
- Equal measurements of any of the following: water, fruit juices, rice milk, soy milk, sunflower seed milk, oat milk, coconut milk

Peanut or other nut butters can be replaced with:
- Equal measurements of either sunflower seed butter or pumpkin seed butter

Butter or margarine can be replaced with:
- Equal measurements of vegan butter, shortening, lard, or coconut oil

Milk on cereal or in coffee/tea/hot chocolate can be replaced with:
- rice milk, soy milk, coconut milk

When accommodating a corn allergy, be sure to avoid using confectioner's sugar that contains corn starch, or oils such as corn oil or vegetable oil. To make your own icing sugar at home, grind white sugar in a coffee grinder in small batches until it becomes powdery in texture.

Common Questions – Answered!

Why do people with food allergies even avoid foods that say "may contain" or "produced in a facility that also produces _"?

When a food is labelled "may contain nuts" for example, or "may contain" any particular allergen, it is safer for the person with food allergies to avoid it altogether as opposed to taking a chance and eating it anyway. In some cases the company may have attached the label to the product for legal liability reasons, but it is impossible to know that just from reading the package. It is very likely that the factory produces both products with and without those allergens. The employees may work with several products in a day, or the machinery may be used to produce several products, increasing risk of cross contamination. In a factory that uses the same equipment for all their products, they may not be able to guarantee that sterilization removed all food residues between uses. If most of their products contain common allergens, it might not be in the best interest of the company to commit to sterilizing and removing all food residues between uses, because the risk of cross contamination is too high. A company cannot package their product with a "made in a peanut/nut - free facility" unless 100% of the products they produce there do not contain those allergens.

Why is a product labelled "allergy friendly" not suitable for all kids with allergies?

Many companies that produce gluten, gluten-, dairy-, or nut-free products, for example, create a brand around "allergy friendliness." In some cases this may work out well for the consumer who has few allergies or whose allergies are among the most common. For example, peanut - free chocolate bars are now readily available in most grocery stores. But just because something is labelled "allergy friendly" that does not mean that the consumer should blindly buy it without first reading the label. Surprisingly, many "allergy friendly" products that are free of dairy or gluten say, may still have a "may contain peanuts or other nuts" warning. It is also important to remember that there are so many common allergens aside from peanuts, nuts, and gluten. The "allergy friendly" product may be a peanut-, nut-, and gluten-free granola bar, but it may be made with egg and butter. As a consumer you have to do your research every time you shop to find out if the product is friendly to *your* allergy.

It is also important to note that when multiple people in a group have food allergies, there can be some conflicts. A common conflict – celiac disease vs. nut and peanut allergy. Because people with celiac disease cannot eat gluten, they often rely on wheat flour substitutes. Common substitutes include almond flour or pea flour; almond flour conflicting with the nut allergy, and pea flour (a legume) possibly conflicting with the peanut allergy if the person is allergic to all legumes. A good alternative that would accommodate both allergies could be coconut or quinoa flour. Another conflict is dairy vs. soy. Many dairy-free products will contain soy milk, coconut milk, or rice milk as a dairy alternative. The problem is that all of these products generally contain soy ingredients. A good alternative that would accommodate both allergies could be fruit juices or even water in most baked goods.

Tips for melting chocolate:

To melt chocolate you can use a double boiler or simply melt it in the microwave. Make sure you have your parents help you because hot chocolate can burn.

A double boiler is the stove-top method. Placing a glass or metal mixing bowl over top of a small pot with one inch of water is a double boiler. The stove should be set to medium - low so that the water is constantly steaming but never boiling. This will heat the bottom of the bowl enough that you can slowly melt the chocolate without burning it. Pour the chocolate chips into the bowl on top of the pot. Lightly stir the chocolate constantly using a wooden or metal spoon until it is smooth and glossy. Then remove the bowl from the heat using oven mitts, and turn the stove off.

Melting chocolate in the microwave is quite simple, but you may need a second pair of hands. Pour the chocolate chips into a medium - sized bowl. Make sure it is microwave safe – no metal bowls! Try to use a wider bowl so that the chocolate is not piled high. If it is spread thinner it will melt more evenly. Do not use a plate because it will be harder to stir and it can be dangerous to take out of the microwave. First microwave it for 45 seconds, and then remove the bowl using oven mitts. Give it a stir with a spoon and then place it in the microwave for an additional 20-35 seconds if it is not yet completely melted. The time will vary for each microwave. Remove it after the additional time and quickly begin to stir it until the chips are totally melted and smooth.

Whichever way you choose to melt chocolate, there are some tips you should keep in mind. Always have oven mitts at the ready because chocolate melts quickly. Melting chocolate is a slow process, so don't try to speed it up by turning up the temperature because it can burn easily. Never use a wet bowl or spoon when touching melted chocolate because it will cause the chocolate to clump together and it will be garbage. Any liquids you want to add to the chocolate (vanilla extract, rice milk, etc.) should be added to the dry chocolate chips before it is put over the heat.

Paring knife
Cookie cutters
Measuring cups
1/4 cup
1/3 cup
1/2 cup
Measuring spoons
Muffin Liners
Piping Tips
Sifter
Whisk
Rolling Pin
a)
b)
Coupler
Grater
:)
Spatula

Kitchen Tools

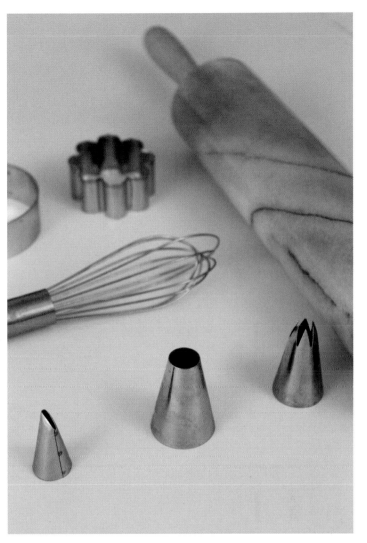

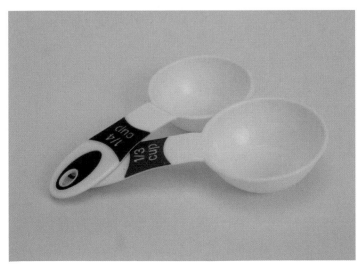

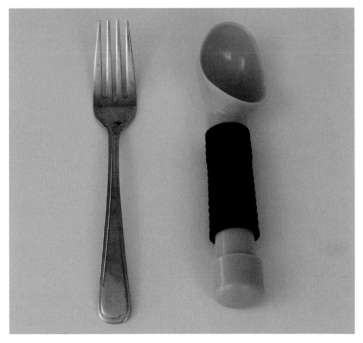

ABOUT THE AUTHOR

Amanda's desire to turn her personal experiences as a person with food allergies into something positive are what led her to write this book. Always ambitious in the kitchen, she has been cooking and baking since the age of 4. When she is not cooking for her boyfriend, friends, or family, she is reading, taming her crazy curly hair, or exploring the city of Toronto, Ontario, where she currently lives with her older brother. She graduated from the University of Toronto in 2012 and now works in publishing.

METRIC AND IMPERIAL CONVERSIONS

(These conversions are rounded for convenience)

Ingredient	Cups/Tablespoons/Teaspoons	Ounces	Grams/Milliliters
Butter	1 cup=16 tablespoons= 2 sticks	8 ounces	230 grams
Cream cheese	1 tablespoon	0.5 ounce	14.5 grams
Cheese, shredded	1 cup	4 ounces	110 grams
Cornstarch	1 tablespoon	0.3 ounce	8 grams
Flour, all-purpose	1 cup/1 tablespoon	4.5 ounces/0.3 ounce	125 grams/8 grams
Flour, whole wheat	1 cup	4 ounces	120 grams
Fruit, dried	1 cup	4 ounces	120 grams
Fruits or veggies, chopped	1 cup	5 to 7 ounces	145 to 200 grams
Fruits or veggies, puréed	1 cup	8.5 ounces	245 grams
Honey, maple syrup, or corn syrup	1 tablespoon	.75 ounce	20 grams
Liquids: cream, milk, water, or juice	1 cup	8 fluid ounces	240 milliliters
Oats	1 cup	5.5 ounces	150 grams
Salt	1 teaspoon	0.2 ounces	6 grams
Spices: cinnamon, cloves, ginger, or nutmeg (ground)	1 teaspoon	0.2 ounce	5 milliliters
Sugar, brown, firmly packed	1 cup	7 ounces	200 grams
Sugar, white	1 cup/1 tablespoon	7 ounces/0.5 ounce	200 grams/12.5 grams
Vanilla extract	1 teaspoon	0.2 ounce	4 grams

OVEN TEMPERATURES

Fahrenheit	Celcius	Gas Mark
225°	110°	¼
250°	120°	¼
275°	140°	1
300°	150°	2
325°	160°	3
350°	180°	4
375°	190°	5
400°	200°	6
425°	220°	7
450°	230°	8

Notes

Notes

Notes

Notes

Notes